The Nature of Man in Early Stoic Philosophy

The Nature of Man in Early Stoic Philosophy

Margaret E. Reesor

St. Martin's Press

New York

© Margaret E. Reesor 1989

First published in the United States of America in 1989

ISBN 0–312–03579–9

Library of Congress Cataloging-in-Publication Data

Reesor, Margaret E.
   The nature of man in early Stoic philosophy / Margaret E. Reesor.
      p.   cm.
   Includes bibliographical references.
   ISBN 0–312–03579–9
   1. Stoics.   2. Man.   3. Philosophical anthropology.   I. Title.
B528.R44   1989
128'.0938—dc20   89–37509
                                                            CIP

Printed in Great Britain

Contents

Preface

About 312 BC Zeno of Citium came to Athens and taught
in the Stoa Poikile. His teachings opened a new era in
philosophical thinking, and the Stoic school that he
founded flourished for more than five hundred years. In
this book I shall confine my investigation to the years
from 312 to approximately 129 BC, the period that was
called by older scholars the Old Stoa. I shall study the
philosophical writings of Zeno of Citium (334 to 262/1
BC), Cleanthes of Assos (*c.* 331/0 to 232/1 BC), Chrysippus
of Soloi, who died between 208 and 204 at the age of 73,
Diogenes of Babylon, who visited Rome in 155, and
Antipater of Tarsus, who was in Rome before 133.[1]

What is the nature of man in Early Stoic Philosophy?
Man is a corporeal *pneuma*, an aggregate of corporeal
qualifications, a single individual quality. He was
brought into being and sustained by the seminal *logos*,
and at his death he will be assimilated into the aether.
Man is also an individually qualified entity, partaking in
both qualification and unqualified matter, whose capacity is realized in a specific society and period.

Above all, man is a being who can utter articulate
sounds, form presentations, make assent to presentations and propositions, and direct his impulse towards

---

[1] For a discussion of the dates of these philosophers see my monograph, *The
Political Theory of the Old and Middle Stoa* (New York, 1951) 1-3; A.A. Long,
Hellenistic Philosophy (London, 1974) 109, 113; and D. Sedley, 'The
Protagonists', in *Doubt and Dogmatism. Studies in Hellenistic Epistemology*,
ed. M. Schofield, M. Burnyeat, J. Barnes (Oxford, 1980) 1-19.

the object of his desire. He can select among the indifferents, and actively choose reasonable activities and virtuous acts. Through a wrong selection among the indifferents, he may form a *doxa* (belief) which is strong enough to divert his impulse away from that which ought to be reasonably desired. The *doxa*, the contraction and elation which follow, and the excessive impulse, are described as emotions. They are disobedient to the *logos* that exercises choice. Man has a prescriptive *logos* ordering what ought to be done and prohibiting the contrary. Through this *logos* man knows the nature of God and acts according to divine law.

Speaking is defined as uttering articulate sound capable of signifying the state of affairs that is conceived. The state of affairs is, of course, the incomplete *lekton*, or predicate. The *lekton* is an intelligible that subsists according to a rational presentation. Since the ruling part of the soul produced the rational presentation according to which the *lekton* subsisted, as well as the articulate sound which signified the predicate, a study of the predicate is a prerequisite for our understanding of the relationship between thought and language in Early Stoic Philosophy.

The Stoics believed that the individual quality, which was both an object of naming, and a term to be defined, was a member of a class of universals. They listed classes of substance and demonstrated their interrelations by diaereses. The distinctions between the corporeal and the incorporeal, substratum and differentiae, were firmly fixed in an all-inclusive ontological system.

Many scholars have helped and encouraged me in my work, and to these I want to express my appreciation now. First, I want to thank the Department of Classics at Princeton University for generously providing me with library facilities and giving me access to a very lively and stimulating program in Ancient Philosophy during the two years when I was a Visiting Fellow in the

Department, 1973-4 and 1980-1. In particular, I want to acknowledge the assistance of David Furley and Michael Frede during my years at Princeton. I only hope that to some degree I may be able to emulate the high quality of their scholarship.

Friedrich Solmsen gave me a great deal of encouragement and advice in my early years when I was a frequent visitor to Cornell, and for this I shall always be grateful. There are other scholars, now gone, whose friendship has meant much to me, and I would like to pay tribute to them now: Lily Ross Taylor, Ludwig Edelstein, B.L. Ullman, Robert Getty, Gwil Owen, and Harold Cherniss. I would like to thank Eric Smethurst for making the Classics Department at Queen's University both pleasant and congenial. It is here that most of my work has been done. Eric's kindnesses are too numerous to be mentioned here, but they will never be forgotten. It is with particular pleasure that I acknowledge my debt to Mr Colin Haycraft, who accepted this book for publication by Gerald Duckworth and Company Ltd, and who, by his diligent reworking of the manuscript, has added much to its form and style. Last of all, I would like to express my gratitude to my mother and my late father whose interest and encouragement over the years meant more to me than words could ever convey.

M.E.R.

1

The Cosmos and the Individual*

Zeno of Citium came to Athens after the death of Xenocrates in 314/3 BC. Polemon was the head of the Academy, and Theophrastus had taken over the Lyceum. A newcomer, Epicurus, was about to found the Garden. Zeno chose to study with Polemon, and had as a fellow student Arcesilaus, the founder of the Sceptical Academy. Although the writings of Theophrastus, Eudemus and Straton show some familiarity with the works of Aristotle, and Epicurus knew the *Analytics*, we cannot say with any assurance that the exoteric works of Aristotle were available to Zeno in Athens.[1] In any case, there is much that Zeno would have rejected in Aristotle's teachings, perhaps most notably the concept of an incorporeal god, and the supposition that the soul was the actualization of the body. Although Zeno used a new term, 'matter', introduced by Aristotle,[2] most of his attention was concentrated on the various aspects of the corporeal body. The nature of God, the soul of man, the

---

* I have cited all references to H. von Arnim, *Stoicorum Veterum Fragmenta*, by the number of the book and fragment, e.g. 2.881.

[1] P. Moraux, *Der Aristotelismus bei den Griechen* (Berlin, 1973) 10-16; F.H. Sandbach, *Aristotle and the Stoics. Cambridge Philological Society* Suppl. 10 (1985) 17, 55-7.

[2] F. Solmsen, 'Aristotle's word for matter', in *Didascaliae. Studies in honor of Anselm M. Albareda* (New York, 1961) 395-408; D.W. Graham, 'Aristotle's discovery of matter', *Arch. Ges. Phil.* 66 (1984) 37-51.

eternity of the cosmos, and the possibility of human knowledge were subjects of intense debate among the rival schools. Zeno, like Aristotle, recognized a close connection between the physical and the psychological.

Although the *pneuma* (air) played a small part in Aristotle's psychology,[3] medical writers, such as Praxagoras of Ceos, Herophilus of Chalcedon and Erasistratus of Ceos, were mainly responsible for the significance that it assumed in early Stoic philosophy.[4] Like Praxagoras, Chrysippus held that the *pneuma* transferred movement from the heart to the sinews,[5] and placed the thought process in the heart.[6] Chrysippus recognized eight parts of the soul, and designated one of these the guiding or ruling part (*hêgemonikon*).[7] The other seven parts are *pneumata*, extending from the ruling part. The five senses are *pneumata* stretching from the ruling part to the organs (2.850, cf. 866); the reproductive part and the vocal part are similarly described (2.836, cf. 841). There was some disagreement about details. Cleanthes, for instance, said that walking was a *pneuma* stretching from the ruling part to the feet, and Chrysippus said that it was the ruling part itself (2.836).

Lapidge has argued persuasively that the concept of cosmic *pneuma* was introduced into Stoic philosophy by Chrysippus, and should not be attributed to Zeno or Cleanthes.[8] Since Solmsen is almost certainly right in

---

[3] D. Ross, *Aristotle. Parva Naturalia* (Oxford, 1970) 40-3.

[4] D.E. Hahm, *The Origins of Stoic Cosmology* (Ohio, 1977) 161-2.

[5] F. Steckerl, *The Fragments of Praxagoras of Cos and his School, Philosophia Antiqua* 8 (Leiden, 1958) F 9, 11, 29, 75.

[6] ibid. F 62, 72.

[7] See F. Adorno, 'Sul significato del termine *hêgemonikon* in Zenone Stoico', *La Parola del Passato. Rivista di Studi Classici* 14 (1959) 26-41.

[8] M. Lapidge, 'A problem in Stoic cosmology', *Phronesis* 18 (1973) 274-6; M. Lapidge, 'Stoic cosmology', in *The Stoics*, ed. J.M. Rist (California, 1978)

attributing the doctrine of *vis caloris*, as it is presented in Cicero's *De Natura Deorum* 2.23-32, to Cleanthes, it is reasonable to assume that heat rather than *pneuma* formed the basis of his cosmology.[9] For Zeno we have evidence for a creative and destructive fire, which sustained the cosmos and was responsible for its conflagration.[10]

The *pneuma* was composed from fire and air (2.310, 442, 786), or the hot and the cold which were equated with fire and air (2.841). The component parts of the *pneuma*, however, were not the elements that formed corporeal matter.[11] The two components of the *pneuma* represented the active and the passive, and corresponded to the seminal *logos* and the prime matter from which the *pneuma* had its source.

The *pneuma*, in its various manifestations throughout the whole cosmos, constituted the world soul, and *aether* was its ruling part (2.634). Just as the other seven parts of the human soul cannot be identified with the ruling

---

169-70. For the Stoic *pneuma* see also G. Verbeke, *L'évolution de la doctrine du pneuma du stoïcisme à S. Augustin* (Paris, 1945); S. Sambursky, *Physics of the Stoics* (London, 1959) 21-48; A.-J. Voelke, *L'idée de volonté dans le stoïcisme* (Paris, 1973) 15-18, 41-3, 104-5; Lapidge (1973) 240-78; Lapidge (1978) 161-85; L. Bloos, *Probleme der Stoischen Physik* (Hamburg, 1973) 52-89; J. Longrigg, 'Elementary physics in the Lyceum and Stoa', *Isis* 66 (1975) 211-29; Hahm (1977).

[9] F. Solmsen, 'Cleanthes or Posidonius? The basis of Stoic physics', in *Kleine Schriften* 1, ed. F. Solmsen (Hildesheim, 1968) 436-60, especially 451-2. For a discussion of the biliography for *De Natura Deorum* 2.24 see M. Dragona-Monachou, *The Stoic Arguments for the Existence and the Providence of the Gods* (Athens, 1976) 96-105.

[10] J. Mansfeld, 'Providence and the Destruction of the Universe in Early Stoic Thought', in *Studies in Hellenistic Religions*, ed. M.J. Vermaseren (Leiden, 1979) 151-8.

[11] When Alexander of Aphrodisias argued that the Stoic *pneuma* was one of the four elements, a mixture of them, or a fifth substance, his conclusion was an inference from his own premise: 'If god is corporeal, and matter is corporeal.' It is not presented as Stoic doctrine (2.130).

part, the *pneuma* itself cannot be identified with the *aether*, although we are told that the *pneuma* and the *aether* fall under the same definition (*logos*, 2.471). The *aether* controls and directs the *pneuma*, just as the ruling part of the human soul controls and directs the other seven parts. The seminal *logos*, that may be called god or *aether*, fabricates the several things (2.134).

The *pneuma* is in constant motion. It is a process into itself, and from itself (2.442). The inward process produces unity and substance, the outward process dimensions and qualities (2.451). The *pneuma* is a disposition (*hexis*) in process (2.634, 458). As a disposition the *pneuma* holds the cosmos together (2.552, 553), and accounts for the cohesions of each individual entity (2.473). The *pneuma* is the cause of the entity's being qualified:

> For the bodies are bound together by these. And the air which binds them together is responsible for each of those things which are bound together by disposition being qualified (*poion*), and they call this air hardness in iron, density in stone and whiteness in silver (2.449).

The qualities are dispositions and fixed dispositions, and consequently *pneumata*. The qualities, 'being *pneumata* and airy tensions, give form and shape to the several things in whatever parts of matter they arise' (2.449).

The *pneuma* is responsible for the qualifications (*poia*) in the corporeal body (*sôma*), whether the qualification is hard or white, a disposition, such as 'being a scholar', or a condition, such as 'being posted in an advanced position'. The *pneuma* is responsible for the conditions of the soul, and the status of the individual, as well as for the physical conditions of the body. A diaeresis in Simplicius not only defines the several kinds of qualification, but provides specifications for some of them (2.390):[12]

[12] For this passage see M.E. Reesor, 'The Stoic categories', *AJP* 78 (1957) 74-7, and '*Poion* and *poiotês* in Stoic philosophy', *Phronesis* 17 (1972) 279-85. See

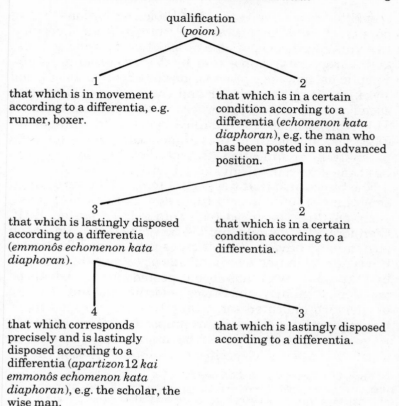

qualification
(*poion*)

1
that which is in movement according to a differentia, e.g. runner, boxer.

2
that which is in a certain condition according to a differentia (*echomenon kata diaphoran*), e.g. the man who has been posted in an advanced position.

3
that which is lastingly disposed according to a differentia (*emmonôs echomenon kata diaphoran*).

2
that which is in a certain condition according to a differentia.

4
that which corresponds precisely and is lastingly disposed according to a differentia (*apartizon* 12 *kai emmonôs echomenon kata diaphoran*), e.g. the scholar, the wise man.

3
that which is lastingly disposed according to a differentia.

Although Simplicius states specifically that the qualification is of three kinds, his discussion indicates the four divisions of the diaeresis above. Two divisions of the diaeresis, 'that which is lastingly disposed according to a differentia' (3) and 'that which corresponds precisely and is lastingly disposed according to a differentia' (4),

also O. Rieth, *Grundbegriffe der Stoischen Ethik* (Berlin, 1933) 22-9 and 171-2. I am grateful to Dr David Sedley for his help in reconstructing this diaeresis.

[13] For *apartizon* see Rieth (1933) 42.

seem to correspond to the Stoic definitions for a possible[14] and a necessary[15] proposition. Diogenes Laertius specifies a possible proposition by 'Diocles lives', and a necessary proposition by 'Virtue benefits' (7.75). Simplicius, however, provides no specification for (3), and specifies (4) by the scholar and the wise man. Diogenes specifies a non-necessary proposition by 'Diocles walks'.[16] This corresponds to qualification (1) in Simplicius' diaeresis, specified by the runner and the boxer, and probably to qualification (2), specified by the man who has been posted in an advanced position.

The Stoics held that the perfect tense of the verb stated something true in present time, and that a perfect tense, such as, 'has been posted' entailed 'is posted'.[17] If, therefore, the definite proposition 'This man has been posted in an advanced position' is true, a qualification of the type designated by Simplicius as (2) may be specified by 'the man who has been posted in an advanced position'. Similarly, the Stoics held that the future tense of the verb indicated something true in present time.[18] Consequently, if the definite proposition 'This man will reign at Corinth' is true, 'the man who will reign at Corinth' is a possible specification for qualification (2).

---

[14] Boethius, *Comm. in Arist. De Interp.* 234,27-9 = 2.201 reads: 'The possible is that which is capable of receiving the predicate true if those things which, although they are external to it, happen to occur with it, do not prevent it.' D.L. 7.75 = 2.201: 'The possible is that which admits of being true if the external circumstances do not prevent it from being true, as, for example, "Diocles lives".'

[15] Boethius, *Comm. in Arist. De Interp.* 235,3-4 = 2.201 reads: 'The necessary is that which, being true, in no way receives the predicate false.' D.L. 7.75 = 2.201: 'The necessary is that which being true, does not admit of being false, or which does admit of it, but external circumstances prevent it from being false, as, for example, "Virtue benefits".'

[16] Boethius does not provide a definition of this term. D.L. 7.75 = 2.201 reads: 'The non-necessary is that which is both true and capable of being false if external circumstances do not prevent it, as, for example, "Dion walks".'

[17] A.C. Lloyd, 'Activity and description in Aristotle and the Stoa', *Proceedings of the British Academy* 56 (1970) 13; C.H.M. Versteegh, 'The Stoic verbal system', *Hermes* 108 (1980) 338-57.

[18] ibid.

It is perfectly conceivable that the same man should be the runner, the boxer, the man who has been posted in an advanced position, the scholar and the wise man. These terms which should properly be specifications for qualified entities (*poioi*) are specifications in Simplicius' diaeresis for qualifications (*poia*). The qualifications are not roles, or aspects of the personality, but fixed dispositions (*diatheseis*, 4), dispositions (*hexeis*, 3), or conditions (*scheseis*, 1 and 2) of the soul. They are corporeal *pneumata* which should be defined in physical terms. A disposition is that 'which can be tightened and loosened', and a fixed disposition is that which is 'neither capable of increase nor diminution'.[19] Sambursky wrote: 'We must realize that the elements of *hexis* are not mere localized units but physical properties which interpenetrate and create a totality where each of them shares in the existence of the rest.'[20] The body which has these dispositions is an aggregate (*athroisma*), a term which Shorey ably defined as: 'a body, viewed not merely as a material aggregate of atoms, but as a metaphysical complex of qualities.'[21]

Although some qualifications, as, for example, the wise man and the scholar, are fixed dispositions of the soul, others, such as the boxer or runner, are conditions which may be lost with advancing age. Others, such as the man who has been posted in an advanced position, have their source in an action at a particular time and in a specific place. A man may acquire a state or condition as the consequence of an action whether he is the perpetrator of it or its recipient. For instance, if Socrates was posted in an advanced position at Delium in 427 BC, his posting depended to a large extent upon circumstances which were outside his control.

[19] Sambursky (1959) 85; cf. A. Graeser, *Zenon von Kition. Positionen und Probleme* (Berlin, 1975) 139, n. 4.
[20] Sambursky (1959) 9.
[21] P. Shorey, 'Plato, Lucretius and Epicurus', *HSCP* 11 (1901) 203.

At a particular moment in time an individual is the totality of his qualifications. These include physical and psychological conditions that he has acquired as the result of his actions or experiences in the past, and conditions that he now possesses which are connected with actions which he may perform or experiences which he may have in the future. Since the world soul is the totality of *pneumata* in the cosmos (2.634), it, like the soul of the individual, existed in time. It too embraced past effects and future possibilities. The world soul, like the individual soul, is a progressive series of patterns in time. It is the function of the soul of the individual to produce qualifications that are individual to him; it is the function of the world soul to produce the qualifications of individuals.

It is inconceivable, therefore, that a man's individuality can be realized in any other society, with any other group of individuals, or in any other period than that in which he is actually living. This interpretation of the qualified entity has far-reaching consequences for the Stoic theory of recurrence. The Stoics held that at regular ten-thousand-year intervals the cosmos experienced a conflagration and the destruction of all existing objects. This was followed by a restoration in which everything was indistinguishable from the former restoration (2.626). Nemesius explains that Socrates, Plato and each of his friends and fellow-citizens will be alive again, and they will have the same experiences, do the same things, and every city, village and field will be reconstituted in the same way (2.625).[22] It is probable, however, that

---

[22] See J. Barnes, 'La doctrine de retour éternel', in *Les stoïciens et leur logique*, ed. J. Brunschwig (Paris, 1978) 3-20; M.J. White, 'Aristotle's temporal interpretation of necessary coming-to-be and Stoic determinism', *Phoenix* 34 (1980) 208-18; Mansfeld (1979) 129-88; A.A. Long, 'The Stoics on world-conflagration and everlasting recurrence', in *Spindel Conference 1984: Recovering the Stoics*, ed. R.H. Epp, *Southern Journal of Philosophy*, vol. 23, suppl. (Memphis, 1985) 13-37, and the review of this chapter by J. Barnes, *Phronesis* 31 (1986) 95.

what appeared in the new cycle was not the individual that had appeared in the previous cycle, but a new individual with the same characteristics and experiences.

At the conflagration, we are told, Zeus, who represents the cosmos, retires into providence, and then both persist in a single substance, aether:

> At any rate, Chrysippus says that Zeus, that is, the cosmos, is like man, and that the providence (*pronoia*) is like his soul; and that, when the conflagration occurs, Zeus who alone of the gods is imperishable, retires into providence and then both, having come together, persist in the single substance, aether (2.1064).

For the cosmos we have the sequence, cosmos, providence, aether, and for man, man, his soul, and presumably, aether. We should be careful, however, not to distinguish the terms providence and aether too arbitrarily. For as Lapidge wrote in his discussion of fire as a creative force: 'Zeno's system was strongly monistic and it would have been equally correct to describe the creative force as *phusis* (nature) or *theos* (god) or even "fate" or "providence".'[23]

Although the cosmos endured through successive rebirths, the soul of the individual did not. Cleanthes held that all souls survived until the conflagration; Chrysippus that only the souls of the wise survived that long (1.552).[24] When the soul was born at the proper time and in the appropriate place in each cycle, a portion of *pneuma*, distinguishable but not separable from unqualified matter, was moved by the seminal *logos*. The soul at this time did not possess any qualifications (*poia*). In fact, 'when a man is born, he has the guiding part of his

---

[23] Lapidge (1973) 254.
[24] J. Bels, 'La survie de l'âme de Platon à Posidonius', *Revue de l'histoire des religions* 199 (1982) 169-82.

soul, just like a papyrus, serviceable for writing' (2.83). When the body of the individual dies, his soul is an aggregate of qualifications. If, therefore, the soul survived until the conflagration, it survived with these qualifications; in other words, it survived with its own individuality.

Why, then, did the Stoics not allow the soul of the individual to survive until its reincarnation in another cycle? The Stoics, we know, rejected the theory of the transmigration of the soul, and the Platonic theory of recollection. They may have thought that, if they acknowledged the survival of the soul until its reincarnation, they would be forced to accept one or both of these theories. On the other hand, they may have concluded that the birth process itself required that that which was being born could not possess the qualifications that it was about to acquire either potentially or actually. To assume that birth was not a real beginning would have led them into hopeless circularity.

According to the doctrine of eternal recurrence, as White stated in his recent article, 'Every event ... would be included in the eternal cyclical temporal nexus'.[25] White, however, also wrote: 'In Lactantius' *Divinae Institutiones* there is an explicit attribution to Chrysippus of the doctrine of the re-establishment of the form of individual persons in successive periods.'[26] Lactantius' statement contradicts the many statements in our ancient sources to the effect that the soul can survive only for a limited period of time and not past the conflagration.[27] It is, therefore, not the same individual who appears in the new cycle, but a new individual.

If what is necessary is the recurrence of specific events

----

[25] White (1980) 213.

[26] The passage in Lactantius reads: 'Since this is the case, it is obvious that it is not impossible that we, after time has elapsed again in a specific cycle, should be restored in the same shape in which we are now' (2.623).

[27] 2.774, 812, 814, 822, and especially 1.147, 1.522.

rather than the re-establishment of the individual entity with its qualifications, there is less fatalism in the system than White supposed. In two earlier articles, I distinguished between initiating and principal causes.[28] The principal cause is part of the nature of the individual. Initiating causes, which are also the antecedent causes of an event (2.952), formed a network of causes external to the principal cause. If only the initiating causes are according to fate (2.933), only the initiating causes form part of the cycle of eternal recurrence. In each cycle, a new individual assumes responsibility for his actions by giving or withholding assent.

At the conflagration, the unqualified matter, that is, the four elements, perishes (D.L.7.134). The *pneuma* survives in the seminal *logos* or god, which is inseparable, although distinguishable from, prime matter.[29] Chrysippus described the seminal *logos* as follows:

He (sc. Chrysippus) said that there were such accounts of an element, that it is that which moves most easily by itself, and the first principle <and the seminal> *logos* and the everlasting power, possessing such a nature that it can move downwards towards [earth,] the point of return, and from the point of return upwards altogether in a circle, consuming all things into itself, and from itself again establishing (sc. them) in an orderly and methodical fashion (2.413).[30]

[28] M.E. Reesor, 'Fate and Possibility in early Stoic philosophy', *Phoenix* 19 (1965) 285-97; M.E. Reesor, 'Necessity and fate in Stoic philosophy', in *The Stoics*, ed. J.M. Rist (California, 1978) 187-202. See also C. Stough, 'Stoic determinism and moral responsibility', in *The Stoics*, 203-31.

[29] Lapidge (1973) 244 quotes Chalcidius *In Tim*. c. 293 Waszink on this point. Cf. *SVF* 2.306, 318, 1054.

[30] Cf. Plut. *Comm. Not.* 1085B: 'And what is more, these men by making god, who is a first principle, an intellectual body and mind in matter ... reveal him as from something else and because of something else.'

The seminal *logos* had two functions: to create the cosmos at the beginning of each cycle, and to receive the cosmos into itself at its end. The creative process, however, was a continuing process that lasted throughout the whole cycle for as long as the *pneuma* permeated unqualified matter. The cosmos was an organism, whole and finite, and the *pneuma* was the life force within it.[31]

In a manner which is reminiscent of Heraclitus and Aeschylus the Stoics held that that which is is good. It is impossible, therefore, to say that any one point in the cycle is better than any other, or that the destruction implicit in the conflagration was to be deplored. God, nature, aether, was the whole cycle, and man was a part of it, both during his sojourn on earth, and his union with the aether.

Every qualified entity (*poios*) had two substrata, the qualification (*poion*) and unqualified matter (*apoios hulê*).[32] The first substratum may be a generic qualification (*koinôs poion*) or an individual qualification (*idiôs poion*, 2.374). In his recent edition of Plutarch's *De Communibus Notitiis*, Cherniss restored 1083D (2.762) to read: 'These men alone saw ... that each of us is two substrata, the one is substance, the other quality (*poiotês*)', but he argued that the word *poiotês* denoted the *idiôs poion* (individual qualification) on the basis of a passage in Arius Didymus: 'For the individual qualification and the substance from which it arises are not the same' (Stob. *Ec.* I, p. 178, 21-179,2).[33]

---

[31] The cosmos was termed 'the whole' and the cosmos together with the infinite void 'the all' (2.522, 523, 524, 525, 535).

[32] In his monumental edition of Posidonius, Theiler collected the evidence for the use of the term 'unqualified matter' in the Stoic tradition. See W. Theiler, *Poseidonios. Die Fragmente* II (Berlin, 1982) 137-8, note on F 257.

[33] H. Cherniss, *Plutarch's Moralia* XIII, part 2 (Harvard, 1976), 850, note b. For a discussion of this passage see M.E. Reesor, 'The Stoic concept of quality', *AJP* 75 (1954) 45-6; J.M. Rist, *Stoic Philosophy* (Cambridge, 1969) 160. Stob. *Ec.* I, p. 178,13-179,2, is quoted in H. Diels, *Doxographi Graeci*[4] (Berlin, 1879,

Plutarch and Arius Didymus attribute change of quantity and quality to the qualification or quality. Plutarch writes:

> The one (i.e. substance) always flows and moves, neither growing larger nor becoming less, nor generally remaining of any character at all, but the other (i.e. quality) remains and grows larger and becomes less and is affected in all respects contrary to the other (2.762).

Arius Didymus states that a qualification (*poion*) receives increase and diminution.[34] Quoting Zeno, however, Diogenes Laertius writes:

> It is described in two ways, as substance and matter, that of the all and that of the particulars. That of the whole does not become more or less, but that of the particulars becomes more and less (1.87).

We are now in a position to say something about the Stoic term corporeal (*sôma*). The Stoics followed Plato (*Soph.* 247D-E) in defining the corporeal as that which can act or be acted upon (1.90) and they called the corporeal that-which-is or Being (*on*, 2.329). The corporeal body is the cause of the attribute and the predicate (1.89), and the latter is a process and an activity. The corporeal body has two constituents, unqualified matter and qualification (2.315). The physical body of a man, his soul, and his particular virtues, are all corporeal bodies, and each of these has the same constituent parts. They differ, however, in their causal properties. The corporeal body receives its individuality and distinguishability from the individual qualification. It is that in which the quality resides.

In a much discussed passage Plutarch wrote:

---

repr. 1965) F 27, pp. 462-3; and L. Edelstein and I.G. Kidd, *Posidonius I. The Fragments* (Cambridge, 1972) F 96, 12-14.

[34] Stob. *Ec.* I p. 178,13-179,2.

> Those are really contrary to the concept, what they say and concoct, that in one substance there are two individually qualified entities (*duo idiôs poioi*), and the same substance having one individually qualified entity takes on a second when it comes upon it, and preserves both alike. For if two, then there will be three, four, five, and more than anyone could tell in a single substance (*Comm. Not.* 1077D = 2.396).

Cherniss argued that this statement is an inference drawn by Plutarch from the statement attributed to Chrysippus which follows, namely that at the conflagration Zeus retires into providence, and both together persist in the single substance, aether.[35] Rist's interpretation is similar.[36] When Plutarch writes: 'in one substance there are two individually qualified entities', he cannot mean that in the same piece of matter there are two separate physical entities, for this would directly contradict a statement in Chrysippus' paradox *Concerning the Growing*: 'Two individually qualified entities cannot be in the same substratum' (2.397). Cherniss, Rist and Sedley have all argued, correctly I believe, that the word substratum in this sentence refers to matter.[37] If, however, the words 'two individually qualified entities' in Plutarch refer to specifications similar to those in Simplicius' diaeresis, as, for example, the runner, the man who has been posted in an advanced position, and the wise man, and not to physically distinct entities, there is no contradiction between the two statements at all.

I agree with Sedley that 'the peculiar quality' (i.e. *idiôs poion*, individual qualification) was 'alone capable of providing living things with continuity of identity'.[38] If,

---

[35] Cherniss (1976) 800 and note c.
[36] Rist (1969) 163-4.
[37] Cherniss (1976) 800; Rist (1969) 163-4; D. Sedley, 'The Stoic criterion of identity', *Phronesis* 27 (1982) 255-75.
[38] Sedley (1982) 261.

therefore, the individual qualification, and not matter, was the principle of individuation, why should not several physically distinct individually qualified entities share a single substratum, matter? To answer this question I shall turn to Chrysippus' paradox *Concerning the Growing* (2.397):

> Let us suppose for the sake of observation that one is whole-limbed and that the other is conceived as lacking one foot, and that the whole-limbed is called Dion, and the one who is incomplete is called Theon, and that afterwards one of the feet of Dion is cut off.
>
> When the question is raised as to which one is destroyed, he (Chrysippus) says that it is more proper for Theon (sc. to be destroyed) ...
>
> Necessarily, Dion, the man whose foot was cut off, springs up into the incomplete substance of Theon, and two individually qualified entities cannot be in the same substratum. Therefore, it is necessary for Dion to remain and for Theon to be destroyed.

The individual qualification (*idiôs poion*), lacking one foot, was the substratum for the individually qualified entity (*ho idiôs poios*), the man lacking one foot. But precisely because the individual qualification was the principle of individuation, each individual qualification could be a substratum for only one individually qualified entity. Therefore, the individual qualification for the individually qualified entity, Dion, when Dion had lost his foot, was not the same as the individual qualification for the individually qualified entity, Theon, who had already lost his foot. Two individually qualified entities cannot be in the same substratum, that is, in the same individual qualification. The matter of the particulars, or unqualified matter, was distinguishable only in thought from the qualification. For every individually qualified entity there was a piece of matter but there was no piece of matter which existed apart from an individually qualified entity.[39] Because it is inseparable from the qualification, the matter of the particulars may be described as having form (D.L. 7.134), and becoming more and less (1.87). Therefore, if two individually qualified entities cannot have a single substratum, the same individual qualification, then they cannot have a single substratum, matter.

The fallacy in the paradox lies in the clause 'springs up into the incomplete substance of Theon'. In Stoic terms this statement is false. If Dion should possess the piece of matter belonging to Theon, he would become Theon, and consequently, Theon would disappear. This, however, is impossible. We should recall that Chrysippus wrote this paradox to support his statement that it is impossible for two individually qualified entities to be in the same substratum. The term 'individually qualified entity' which was used to describe the musician or the athlete is here used to refer to a separable, physical entity. The same man may be a musician, professor and athlete but he cannot become another discrete entity.

For the specification in divisions (1), (2), (3) and (4) of Simplicius' diaeresis we may construct two substrata: qualification (*poion*) and unqualified matter (*apoios hulê*). Only in (3) and (4), however, does the qualification correspond to the quality. Simplicius writes: 'Therefore, when they define the quality as a disposition of the qualification (*schesin poiou*), we must understand by this that the third kind (our 3 and 4) of quality is meant' (2.390).

In conclusion, I shall discuss the evidence for the individual quality. What was the individual quality? Was there an individual quality 'Socrates' which was the cause of the attribute 'being Socrates' and the predicate 'is Socrates' in the proposition 'This man is Socrates'? From a passage in Plutarch we learn that a virtue was an individual quality:

---

[39] Cherniss (1976) 800.

Chrysippus, believing that a virtue was formed by its own individual quality (*idia poiotês*) according to the qualification (*kata to poion*), unconsciously aroused in Plato's words, 'a swarm of virtues', which were not customary or familiar. From a comparison with the courageous man he introduced courage, from a comparison with the gentle man gentleness (3.255).

All of the qualified entities mentioned in this passage, the courageous man, the gentle man, the righteous man, the graceful man, the good man, are specifications for qualifications (3), that is, *poion* (3), in Simplicius' diaeresis. Since the corresponding quality is an individual quality, each of these entities is an individually qualified entity (*idiôs poios*). From the individually qualified entity Chrysippus inferred the existence of the corresponding individual quality.

At the same time Zeno and presumably Chrysippus regarded the quality in a particular entity as the cause of an attribute of the entity and a predicate:

> Zeno says that a cause is that 'because of which'; and that that for which there is a cause is an attribute (*sumbebêkos*). And that the cause is a *sôma* (corporeal body), and that that for which there is a cause is a predicate (*katêgorêma*) ... A cause is that because of which something happens, as, for example, thinking wisely (*to phronein*) arises because of practical wisdom (*phronêsis*), and living (*to zên*) because of soul (*psuchê*), and acting moderately (*to sôphronein*) because of moderation (*sôphrosunê*, *Ec.* I, p. 138, 14-20 = 1.89).[40]

Because of the presence of wisdom, a man possesses the attribute 'thinking wisely', and is able to say of himself 'I am thinking' (1.89). The quality is the cause of *x*, for example, 'thinking wisely' in the entity *y*. Frede defined the Stoic cause as 'a body which does something

---

[40] For a discussion of this passage see Graeser (1975) 82-9.

or other and by doing so brings it about that another body
is affected in such a way that something comes to be true
of it'.[41] Practical wisdom, soul, and moderation were all
corporeal. This is clear not only from the passage in
Stobaeus mentioned above but from a passage in
Plutarch which reads:

> For it is very absurd of them to make the virtues and the
> vices and the skills and all the memories besides and
> presentations, moreover, and affections and impulses and
> assents corporeal, and to say that they do not reside or
> are real in anything (*Comm. Not.* 1084A).

Cherniss explained that, since they were all dispositions
of the soul, and the soul was corporeal, they were all
corporeal.[42]

The terms *sôma* (corporeal body) and *poion* (qualification) are carefully distinguished by Diogenes Laertius
and Aetius. Diogenes writes: 'A notion (*ennoêma*) is an
impression of a mind, neither being something (*ti*) nor a
qualification, but some kind of something and some kind
of qualification, as, for example, the likeness of a horse
which arises if a horse is not present' (3.25). Aetius
argues that the forms are our notions (2.360). Alexander
of Aphrodisias describes 'something' as predicated not
only of corporeals but of incorporeals as well (2.329).[43]

Although a term, such as *epistêmê* (exact knowledge)
could be both a *poion* (qualification), and a *sôma*
(corporeal body), and a quality, such as *phronêsis*
(practical wisdom) could be both a *poiotês* (quality) and a

[41] M. Frede, 'The original notion of cause', in *Doubt and Dogmatism. Studies in
Hellenistic Epistemology*, ed. M. Schofield, M. Burnyeat, J. Barnes (Oxford,
1980) 234.

[42] Cherniss (1976) 855, and 854, note d. For the corporeal see I. Mueller,
'Geometry and scepticism', in *Science and Speculation*, ed. J. Barnes *et al.*
(Cambridge, 1982) 74-7.

[43] For 'something' see Rist (1969) 153-4; and P. Pasquino, 'Le statut
ontologique des incorporels dans l'ancien stoïcisme', in *Les stoïciens et leur
logique*, 375-86.

sôma (corporeal body), the terms qualification or quality and corporeal body were not interchangeable. The qualification was a condition, a disposition, or exact disposition. It could not exist independently of the substratum. The corporeal body, on the other hand, was a substratum, and could exist independently of a particular qualification, but not of all qualifications. The qualities could, in fact, be either corporeal or incorporeal: 'The Stoics say that the qualities of the corporeals are corporeal and the qualities of the incorporeals are incorporeal' (Simpl. *In Cat.* p. 217,32-3). The incorporeal qualifications may have been called *hekta* (habits, 2.461).[44]

Passages in Stobaeus provide a good deal of evidence for the formation of the individual quality from the qualification and the essential characteristic (*idion*):

Each of these (sc. virtues) makes it possible for a man to provide for himself through the essential characteristics. For he has a starting point from his own nature with respect to the finding of the appropriate act, the stability of the impulses, endurance and distribution (*Ec.* II, p. 62,8-12).

For the chief essential characteristic of moderation is to provide for oneself impulses that are stable and to observe them primarily, and secondly, (sc. to observe) these (sc. essential characteristics) which belong to the other virtues (*Ec.* II, p. 63,15-18).

For the individual quality, wisdom, we may reconstruct the qualification and the essential characteristic as follows:

---

[44] For the *hekton* see Rieth (1933) 56.

poion (qualification)	*idion* (essential characteristic)	*idia poiotês* (individual quality)
epistêmê (exact knowledge)	*pros tên tou kathêkontos heuresin* (with respect to the finding of the appropriate act)	*phronêsis* (practical wisdom)[45]

Simplicius defines the qualification (*poion*) as 'everything that is according to a differentia' (2.390). Since the relations, which he specifies by sweet, bitter, disposition (*hexis*), exact knowledge (*epistêmê*) and perception (*aisthêsis*) are according to a differentia (2.403), these specifications are necessarily qualifications.

Although it is easy to distinguish the qualification from the individual quality, the distinction between the individual qualification and the individual quality is not as clear. Although Plutarch names two substrata, substance and quality (*Comm. Not.* 1083D = 2.762), Arius Didymus refers to the individual qualification and the substance from which it arises (Stob. *Ec.* I, p. 178,13-179,2). The two terms, individual quality and individual qualification, seem to be used synonymously. The naming of the individual, however, was the naming of the individual quality, for Diogenes of Babylon defines the common noun as 'a part of a *logos*, signifying a common quality, as, for example, "man", "horse",' and a proper name (*onoma*), as 'a part of a *logos*, indicating an individual quality (*idia poiotês*), as, for example, "Diogenes", "Socrates" ' (3.22). The term to be defined was either an individual quality or an individual qualification. Chrysippus defined a definition as 'the assigning of the essential characteristic' (2.226). This was the assigning of the essential characteristic, we may suppose, to the qualification. We may conclude, there-

---

[45] For a further discussion of this topic see M.E. Reesor, 'The Stoic *idion* and Prodicus' near-synonyms', *AJP* 104 (1983) 127.

fore, that the individual, Socrates, possessed an individual quality, which presumably included a very large number of individual qualifications, both essential and accidental, and that this individual quality was a corporeal cause of the attribute 'being Socrates', and of the predicate 'is Socrates' in a proposition, such as 'This is Socrates.'

What is the nature of the individual in early Stoic philosophy? He is corporeal *pneuma*, an aggregate of corporeal qualifications, a single individual quality. He was brought into being and sustained by the seminal *logos*, and at his death he will be assimilated into the aether. A new individual, identical to him in all respects, will appear in the new cycle. Man is also an individually qualified entity, partaking in both qualification and unqualified matter, whose capacity is realized in a specific society and period, and preserved in the aether.

2

Stoic Ontology

In recent articles, Graeser has argued that in early Stoic philosophy individual qualities were 'incorporeal meanings',[1] and that the Stoic categories were 'classifications of meaning'.[2] In this chapter I propose to re-examine the evidence for Stoic ontology, and to consider the role of nominalism in Stoic philosophy.[3]

Krämer collected the evidence for 'classes of Being' (*genê tôn ontôn*) in the writings of Plato and the Academy.[4] The Stoic diaereses that I am going to investigate certainly belong to this tradition. Since Being (*on*) for the Stoics was predicated only of the corporeals (2.329), the Stoic classification was a classification of 'something' (*ti*), a term predicated of the corporeals and incorporeals alike (ibid.). In our first diaeresis, the classes are classes of substance; they are interdependent, and their numbers are exhaustive. Since the passage is

---

[1] A. Graeser, 'The Stoic categories', in *Les stoïciens et leur logique*, ed. J. Brunschwig (Paris, 1978) 205.

[2] ibid. 206.

[3] For nominalism in Stoic philosophy see also G. Verbeke, 'Der Nominalismus der stoischen Logik', *Allgemeine Zeitschrift für Philosophie* 11,3 (1977) 36-55. For a useful discussion of nominalism see P. Vignaux, 'La problématique du nominalisme médiéval peut-elle éclairer des problèmes philosophiques actuels?', *Revue philosophique de Louvain* 75 (1977) 293-331.

[4] H.J. Krämer, *Platonismus und Hellenistische Philosophie* (Berlin, 1971) 82-107. See also for a discussion of Platonic ontology J.M. Moravcsik, 'Recollecting the theory of Forms', in *Facets of Platonic Philosophy*, ed. W.H. Werkmeister (Van Gorcum, 1976) 1-20.

important, a translation and commentary seem to be required:

(a) The Stoics say that the 'common of quality' (*to koinon tes poiotêtos*) (b) which pertains to the corporeals (*to epi tôn sômatôn*) is a differentia of substance, not apprehensible by itself, (c) but reaching its acme in one thought and individuality (*eis hen noêma kai idiotêta apolêgousan*), (d) not formed by time or force but by its own particularity according to which the genesis of the qualification subsists (*têi ex autês toioutotêti kath' hên poiou huphistatai genesis*). But in this, if it is not possible according to their account, that (e) there should be a common property of corporeals and incorporeals (*koinon sumptôma sômatôn kai asômatôn*), the quality will no longer be a genus (2.378).

(a) 'The common' is that in which two or more activities or objects participate, and which for that reason may be said to be common to both. For instance, healing is common to the doctor and the layman (3.516). Good things are common to the man who benefits and the one who is benefited (3.94). I would, therefore, define 'the common of quality' as that which is common to all the members of the diaeresis of quality.

(b) Two examples from Plato may serve to indicate the possible connotations of the term *epi*. In the *Protagoras*, Plato writes: 'Are not all actions which pertain to this (*epi toutou*), to living painlessly and pleasantly, fine?' (358b3-5). In the *Republic*, however, Plato uses the word *epi* to mean 'over' or 'in charge' in the phrase 'officials appointed in charge of these things' (460b8). The word may, therefore, be translated as 'over' or 'pertains to'.

(c) I have accepted von Arnim's *eis hen noêma* (in one thought) in preference to Kalbfleisch's *eis ennoêma* (in supposition). The word *noêma* (thought) might reasonably refer to the *koinôs poion* (generic qualification), and *idiotês* (individuality) to the *idiôs poion* (individual qualification). The term *noêma* (thought) may have been corporeal, since it is not listed among Sextus Empiricus' four incorporeals (2.331). We are specifically told that the *ennoêmata* (suppositions) are not 'some things (*tina*)' (1.65). Since the term *ti* (something) was predicated of both corporeals and incorporeals, the *ennoêmata* (suppositions) hardly belong to a passage whose subject is 'the common of quality that pertains to the corporeals' (2.378).

(d) The 'common of quality' is formed by its own particularity, and the genesis of the qualification subsists according to this. The genesis of the qualification is a function of the seminal *logos* that fabricates all things.

(e) The term 'common property of corporeals and incorporeals' is mentioned in another passage in Simplicius (*In Cat.* p. 216,19-27):

> What is more, if some people form the qualities from 'what are usually termed predicates', as, for example, in the case of those things that are real according to the common property of corporeals and incorporeals alike, as, for example, from being roofed, roofing, and from having been made equal, equality, and from the fact that the corporeal is real, corporeality, they do not declare this correctly. For dispositions (*hexeis*) do not owe their reality to the concurrence of predicates, as, for example, when 'being separate' is characteristic of columns, 'separation' is not visualized in their regard because of this. For the predicate which is only observed in speaking can be observed in the case of those things which are not subsistent.

Terms such as roofing, equality and corporeality, subsist according to 'the common property of corporeals and incorporeals', a term which is prior to 'the common of quality'. Since they do not subsist according to 'the common of quality', they are not qualifications (*poia*), or dispositions (*hexeis*). The 'common of quality' and the 'common property of corporeals and incorporeals' must in some sense have played a role similar to the paradigm in Plato's *Timaeus*.

We should now construct a diaeresis which reads:

the common property of corporeals and incorporeals (*ti*)

the common of quality that per-   the incorporeals
tains to the corporeals

thoughts   individuality   the expressible (*lekton*)
(common   (individual   (e.g. the predicate)
qualifications)   qualifications)

According to Sextus Empiricus, there are four incorporeals: *lekton* (expressible), *kenon* (void), *topos* (place), *chronos* (time, 2.331). There is evidence that void and place were conceived by reflection (*epinoia*). Cleomedes states that the 'reflection of void was very simple, that it was incorporeal, and impalpable, and neither had shape nor was shaped, and neither suffered anything nor acted upon anything, but simply was such as to receive body' (2.541). Simplicius similarly says that 'place subsists with bodies and receives its definition from them inasmuch as it is filled by bodies' (2.507). What Simplicius called a definition was presumably the essential characteristic (2.226). It is reasonable to suppose that all four incorporeals were conceived by reflection. The terms roofing, equality, and corporeality are formed from the expressibles. I am at a loss to know what they were called. Since the genus 'something' (*ti*) was predicated not only of corporeals but of incorporeals as well (2.329), we may assume that 'the common property of corporeals and incorporeals' was 'something'.

Simplicius refers to both corporeals and incorporeal qualities: 'The Stoics say that the qualities of the corporeals are corporeal and the qualities of the incorporeals are incorporeal' (*In Cat.* p. 217,32-3). The word *hexis* (disposition) seems to have been used to describe the disposition of the corporeal, and the term *hekton* to indicate the disposition of the incorporeal (2.461).

The qualifications (*poia*), and the relative dispositions (*pros ti pôs echonta*) appear in a diaeresis in Simplicius which is described as follows:

> The Stoics, instead of one genus, number two in this topic, placing some in relations (*ta pros ti*), others in relative dispositions (*ta pros ti pôs echonta*). And they distinguish logically relations from things in themselves (*ta kath' hauta*) and relative dispositions from things according to the differentia (*ta kata diaphoran*), calling relations the sweet and bitter and such things and whatever disposes in such a way, and calling relative dispositions right and father and other such things (*In Cat.* p. 165,32-8 = 2.403).[5]

things in themselves	relations
(*ta kath' hauta*)	(*ta pros ti*)
things according to a differentia	relative dispositions
(*ta kata diaphoran*)	(*ta pros ti pôs echonta*)

If, therefore, we combine this diaeresis with the one that I constructed above, we have two prior terms for things according to a differentia, that is, the qualifications (*poia*):

the common of quality	relations
(*to koinon tês poiotêtos*)	(*ta pros ti*)

things according to a differentia
(*ta kata diaphoran*)

---

[5] For this passage see O. Rieth, *Grundbegriffe der Stoischen Ethik* (Berlin, 1933) 70-84, 190-1; M.E. Reesor, 'The Stoic categories', *AJP* 78 (1957) 72-7; Krämer (1971) 85; Graeser (1978b) 208-11; P. Moraux, *Der Aristotelismus bei den Griechen* (Berlin, 1973) 158 suggests that Simpl. *In Cat.* p. 165,32-166,29 was based on Boethus.

What are usually called the Stoic categories are an ontological classification of the *sôma* (corporeal body).[6] They are listed in Simplicius and Plotinus as: substratum (*hupokeimena*), qualification (*poia*), disposition (*pôs echonta*), and relative disposition (*pros ti pôs echonta*).[7] For instance, the ruling part of the soul (*hêgemonikon*), a corporeal body, is a substratum, and the ruling part of the soul in a certain disposition (*pôs echon*) is exact knowledge (*epistêmê*).[8] Exact knowledge, however, is a specification for 'that which is disposed according to a differentia', which, in turn, is a qualification (2.403, 2.390). The term *epistêmê* (exact knowledge), therefore, is both a corporeal body, since the ruling part of the soul is a corporeal body, and a qualification. If we carry this further, we find that exact knowledge, a qualification, with the addition of the essential characteristic, is an individual quality, a virtue, as, for example, practical wisdom. The virtue, practical wisdom, in turn, is a corporeal body, because the qualification, exact knowledge, is a corporeal body, and an individual quality.

The fourth category, relative disposition, is a species of relation (*pros ti*). According to Simplicius, 'It is observed ... according to its bare relation to something else' (2.403). It was probably of more significance than the specifications 'father', 'son', 'right', and 'left' would indicate (2.403).

Graeser believed that the individual qualities were 'incorporeal meanings', and the Stoic categories were 'classifications of meaning'. He wrote:

---

[6] For the Stoic categories see Rieth (1933) 70-91; P.H. De Lacy, 'The Stoic Categories as Methodological Principles', *TAPA* 76 (1946) 246-63; Reesor (1957) 63-82; J.M. Rist, *Stoic Philosophy* (Cambridge, 1969) 152-72; Krämer (1971) 95; J.M. Rist, 'Categories and their Uses', in *Problems in Stoicism*, ed. A.A. Long (London, 1971) 38-57; Graeser (1978b) 199-221.

[7] Simpl. *In Cat.* p. 67,1-2 = *SVF* 2.369, Plot. VI.1.25 = 2.371.

[8] S.E. *Math.* 7.39. For a discussion of the category 'in a certain disposition' (*pôs echon*) see M. Pohlenz, 'Zenon und Chrysipp', *Nach. Ges. Wiss. Göttingen Phil.-hist. Kl.* 2, 9 (1938) 184-5.

Accordingly, when Diogenes (sc. of Babylon) is said to
have held that proper names indicate individual qualities
it seems reasonable to suppose that he did not mean to
claim that proper names denote qualities but held that
the qualities under consideration are incorporeal meanings alike signified along with their reference.[9]

Graeser followed Lloyd[10] in holding that what are
usually called the Stoic categories were 'classifications of
basic types of meaning'.[11] Lloyd and Graeser argued that
the demonstrative pronoun (*arthron*) corresponded to the
substratum, the proper name (*onoma*) and the common
noun (*prosêgoria*) to the qualifications (*poia*), the verb
(*rhêma*) to the disposition, and the 'transitive verb'
(*sundesmos*) to the relative disposition.[12]

Graeser referred to the divisions of Simplicius'
diaeresis (*In Cat.* p. 165, 32-8 = 2.403) as 'ontological
constituents',[13] and the categories as 'classifications of
different expressions denoting the same objects'.[14] His
inability to give the qualifications and the relative
dispositions similar descriptions in the two passages
weakens his case for interpreting the categories as
'classifications of expressions'.

Graeser's interpretation directly contradicts Plotinus'
statement that the Stoic categories were four 'classes of
Being' (2.371). He attempts to explain the discrepancy by
saying:

[9] Graeser (1978b) 205.

[10] A.C. Lloyd, 'Grammar and metaphysics in the Stoa', in *Problems in
Stoicism*, 66.

[11] Graeser (1978b) 206.

[12] Lloyd (1971) 66-9; A. Graeser, *Zenon von Kition. Positionen und Probleme*
(Berlin, 1975) 16-18; A. Graeser, 'The Stoic theory of meaning', in *The Stoics*,
ed. J.M. Rist (California, 1978a) 78-9; Graeser (1978b) 206-7; A. Graeser, 'On
language, thought and reality in Ancient Greek philosophy', *Dialectica* 31
(1977) 380-1.

[13] Graeser (1978b) 214.

[14] ibid.

As referred to and dealt with by both Plotinus and Simplicius the so-called categories are introduced as proto-Aristotelian classifications, as though they were meant to furnish natural classes of entities answering to the different kinds of words through which we approach reality. In other words, they are placed within the framework of what may be called a realist theory of meaning.[15]

Graeser goes on to say: 'The Stoics did not hold a realist theory of meaning.'[16] At this point I find myself in complete disagreement with Graeser's statement.

Graeser carried his argument further in an article in *Dialectica*.[17] Here he drew attention to a passage in which Diogenes Laertius, after referring to Zeno, Cleanthes, Chrysippus, Archedemus and Posidonius, wrote:

They say that the first principles and elements are different, that the former do not come into being <and> pass away, but that the elements are destroyed at the conflagration. Moreover, that the first principles are incorporeal (*asômatous*) and without form (*amorphous*), but the latter have form (7.134 = 2.299).

There has been a great deal of discussion regarding this sentence. Most of the manuscripts read *sômata*. The reading *asômatous* is based on an emendation of Suidas, and was accepted by Long in the Oxford edition of Diogenes Laertius. Lapidge,[18] Hahm[19] and Kerferd[20] have argued in favor of *sômata*. Graeser and Theiler

[15] ibid. 202.
[16] ibid. 203.
[17] Graeser (1977) 378.
[18] M. Lapidge, 'A problem in Stoic cosmology', *Phronesis* 18 (1973) 263-4.
[19] D.E. Hahm, *The Origins of Stoic Cosmology* (Ohio, 1977) 32, 49 n.12.
[20] G.B. Kerferd, 'The origin of evil in Stoic thought', *Bulletin of the John Rylands University Library of Manchester* 60 (1978) 484.

supported *asômatous*, but saw the influence of Posidonius in this passage.[21]

I believe that the resolution of the problem depends
upon the interpretation of the elements. The function of
the first two principles was to produce the elements,
which were identical with unqualified matter: 'He (sc.
god) produces first the four elements, fire, water, air and
earth ... The four elements together are the unqualified
substance' (7.136-7). If the elements are indeed unqualified substance, the first principles from which they were
formed must necessarily be incorporeal.

In *Dialectica* Graeser comments on Posidonius'
incorporeal first principles as follows: 'In other words,
while traditional ontology proceeded from the tacit
assumption that terms like "matter", "form", "God", and
"principle" have genuine denotations, the Stoics thought
of them as indicating meanings and providing contri-
butions of functional thought.'[22] The term 'incorporeal'
(*asômatos*) is not synonymous with 'meaning'. When
Posidonius used the term 'incorporeal' to describe the
first principles, he was describing the first principles as
'without body', that is, as lacking the essential
characteristic of body 'to be such that it can act and be
acted upon'.[23] The incorporeal and the corporeal together
constituted the ontological 'something' (*ti*).

In the next chapter I shall attempt to refute Graeser's
charge that 'the Stoics claimed that there is no body
corresponding to the thing meant',[24] or 'they were the
first to realize that there was no body corresponding to
our statements'.[25] I shall argue that the predicate in a
true proposition corresponded to the attribute and that

[21] Graeser (1975) 107. W. Theiler, *Poseidonios. Die Fragmente* II (Berlin,
1982) 137-8, note on F 257.

[22] Graeser (1977) 378.

[23] See also R. Renehan, 'On the Greek origins of the concepts incorporeality
and immateriality', *Greek, Roman and Byzantine Studies* 21 (1980) 105-38.

[24] Graeser (1977) 378.

[25] ibid. 386.

the attribute and the predicate together had their source in a common corporeal body. We cannot conclude from the fact that Stoic physics conceived the total sum of existence in terms of a moving continuum that 'our mind divides and articulates reality, arriving at logical constituents even where the physical components are inseparable'.[26] The evidence simply does not support this kind of nominalism.

---

[26] ibid. 382.

3

The Predicate in Early Stoic Philosophy

In Stoic epistemology the predicate is much more than a verbal form attached to a case. It is a state of affairs and an activity. It has a corporeal body as its cause, and it shares this cause with a corresponding attribute. Since it subsisted according to a rational presentation, it bridged the gap between its source, a corporeal body, and the presentation which is apprehended in the thinking process. Further, since the ruling part of the soul produced the rational presentation according to which it subsisted, as well as the articulate sound which signified the predicate, a study of the predicate is a prerequisite for our understanding of the relationship between thought and language in early Stoic philosophy.

The word *katêgorêma* in Aristotle had the meaning 'predicate'.[1] For convenience, I shall use this translation in my discussion of the term. There is some doubt, however, whether the word had this meaning in the teachings of the Stoics. Hamlyn in his article 'Aristotle on Predication' writes: 'The use of the phrase *katêgorein ti kata tinos* stems from legal contexts; it thus comes to mean "maintain or assert something of something", and it perhaps retains something of an accusatorial aura.'[2]

---

[1] Arist. *De Interp.* 20b32, *Met.* 1053b19.
[2] D.W. Hamlyn, 'Aristotle on predication', *Phronesis* 6 (1961) 110.

The verb *katêgoreô*, moreover, is used in Aeschylus' *Agamemnon* with the meaning 'signify' or 'indicate' (271); and the noun *katêgoros* in the *Seven against Thebes* has the meaning 'indicator' or 'signifier' (438-9). Many words which are familiar in the plays of Aeschylus appear in Stoic philosophy.[3] The ending *-êma* in the word *katêgorêma* indicates that the noun is the end or result of an action.[4] It is the end which follows from the action of signifying (*katêgorein*) and should properly be translated as 'signification'.

That which signifies in the Stoic theory of language is a *logos*. It is defined by Diogenes of Babylon as 'articulate sound capable of signifying, sent forth from a mind' (D.L. 7.56 = 3.20, p. 213). According to Chrysippus and Diogenes of Babylon, there are five parts of this *logos*, proper name, common noun, verb, transitive verb, and pronoun (D.L. 7.57 = 3.21). Only three of these signify: the proper name indicates the individual quality, the common noun signifies the common quality, and the verb signifies a predicate (D.L. 7.58 = 3.22).[5]

For the Stoics speaking was 'speaking a *pragma* (state of affairs) that happened to be expressible'. When we speak, we speak predicates, as, for example, 'He is listening', or predicates and cases, as, for example, 'He is speaking to Socrates'. We do not speak nouns and verbs. This is made perfectly clear by Diogenes of Babylon when he writes:

[3] See W. Burkert, 'La genèse des choses et des mots. Le papyrus de Derveni entre Anaxagore et Cratyle', *Les études philosophiques* (1970) 448, n. 3.

[4] M.H. Bonitz, 'Über *Pathos* und *Pathêma* im Aristotelischen Sprachgebrauche', *Akad. der Wiss. Wien. Sitz.* 55 (1867) 18.

[5] With the exception of a few fragments, the evidence for the theory of language held by Diogenes of Babylon is to be found in Diogenes Laertius' *Lives of the Philosophers*, 7.49-82. In his *Stoicorum Veterum Fragmenta*, XXX-XLIII, von Arnim argued that this part of Diogenes' treatise was an excerpt from the *Survey of the Philosophers* written by Diocles of Magnesia in the first century BC. Recently, in his discussion of this passage, Mejer wrote that the most likely conclusion was that the Stoic doxography could not have been composed by Diogenes himself, and must have been taken from some

> Speaking (*legein*) is different from uttering (*propheresthai*), for the articulate sounds are uttered but the *pragmata* (states of affairs) that happen to be *lekta* (expressibles) are spoken (D.L. 7.57 = 3.20).

The sentence in Sextus Empiricus which reads:

> Speaking is, as the Stoics say, uttering articulate sound, capable of signifying the state of affairs that is conceived (*tou nooumenou pragmatos, Math.* 8.80 = 2.167)

does not contradict Diogenes' statement. Diogenes is describing what is spoken, namely, the *pragmata* (states of affairs) that happen to be expressible, and Sextus Empiricus is indicating the means by which the expressibles are spoken, uttering articulate sound. The function of the verb is to signify the predicate; a predicate is that which we speak, and the predicate when combined with a case is a proposition.

Passages in Diogenes Laertius provide evidence that the predicate was regarded as a *pragma* (state of affairs). Diogenes Laertius defined the verb as follows:

> A verb (*rhêma*) is a part of a *logos* signifying an uncompounded predicate, as Diogenes (sc. of Babylon) says, or, as some say, an element of a *logos*, not joined to any case, signifying *something constructed about something or some things*, as, for example, 'I write', 'I speak' (D.L. 7.58 = 3.22).

It is clear from Diogenes' definition of the predicate that the words that I italicized above refer to the *pragma*:

> The predicate is that which is predicated about something, either a *pragma constructed about something or some things*, as Apollodorus and his followers say, or a

---

other source. J. Mejer, *Diogenes Laertius and his Hellenistic background Hermes Einzelschriften* 40 (1978) 6-7.

deficient *lekton* (expressible) combined with a nominative case to generate a proposition (D.L. 7.64 = 2.183).

The first definition, namely that the predicate is a *pragma*, a state of affairs, is attributed to Apollodorus and his followers. A passage in Clement of Alexandria indicates that this was the general view: 'the causes are (sc. causes) of predicates, or, *as some say*, of expressibles (*lekta*), for Cleanthes and Archedemus call the predicates expressibles' (*SVF* 3.8, p. 263).

The proposition (*axiôma*) is composed of a case (*ptôsis*) and a predicate (*katêgorêma*, Plut. *Quaest. Plat.* 1009C). Since Chrysippus regarded the proposition as a *pragma* (D.L. 7.65), we may assume that he defined the predicate as a state of affairs.

Kerferd drew attention to a passage in the Scholia to Lucian's *Philosophers for Sale*, and translated part of the passage as follows:

> But the Stoics, being people who make a display of accuracy and who like to use strange words, for their part say that a complete proposition, such as, 'Socrates walks' is an occurrence (*sumbama*) or a predicate. For 'walking' is something that has happened to Socrates.[6]

Commenting on this passage, Kerferd wrote: 'For the Stoics there was a sense in which a whole statement could be regarded as predicated of the situation in the real world ... Instead, it possesses an extra-linguistic reference to what is the case.'[7]

In the passage in Clement of Alexandria to which I

---

[6] *Scholia in Lucianum*, ed. H. Rabe (Stuttgart, 1906, repr. 1971) 128,18-129,16.

[7] G.B. Kerferd, 'Two problems concerning impulses', in *On Stoic and Peripatetic Ethics. The Work of Arius Didymus*, ed. W.W. Fortenbaugh, *Rutgers University Studies in Classical Humanities* 1 (1982) 95-6. For *pragma* see also D.L. Blank, *Ancient Philosophy and Grammar. American Classical Studies* 10 (Chico, California, 1981) 22.

referred above, predicates are described as activities: 'Coming-to-be and being-cut, for which there are causes, although they are activities (*energeiai*), are incorporeal' (3.8, p. 263). The little that we know about the Stoic concept of activity is found in Simplicius, in a passage which reads:

> For when the Stoics speak of the differentiae of the classes they say (1) *to ex hautôn kineisthai* (process originating in themselves), as, for example, the knife has 'cutting' from its own constitution (for the procedure is completed according to its character and form); (2) *to di' heautou energein, tên kinêsin* (acting through oneself, the process), just as the various kinds of nature and the medical powers function. For the seed when it is deposited completes the related measures and attracts the available matter and shapes the measures in it. (3) And further, *to aph' heautou poiein* (functioning from oneself), which is, generally, functioning from an individual impulse, and something different from functioning from a rational impulse, which is described by the term 'effecting';[8] acting in accordance with virtue (*to kat' aretên energein*) is a species of this (2.499).

In another passage in Simplicius, however, we find the statement:

> As Iamblichus says, the Stoics incorrectly apprehend the process (*kinêsis*) when they say that the incompleteness which pertains to the process is agreed upon, not because it is an activity, for it certainly is an activity, they say, but its action is repeated not in order that it may attain to an activity, for it is one already, but in order that it may effect something else which follows upon it (2.498).

---

[8] Reading *prattein* for *plattein*. See B. Inwood, *Ethics and Human Action in Early Stoicism* (Oxford, 1985) 262, n. 22. See also O. Rieth, *Grundbegriffe der Stoischen Ethik. Problemata* 9 (Berlin 1933) 127-33. For a comparison with *SVF* 2.989, see Inwood, 22-5.

Although (1) and (2) in Simplicius' classification (2.499), may be said to 'effect something else which follows upon it' only (1) can be described as an action which is repeated. This raises the question whether (2) should be described as a process at all.

The three kinds of activities listed by Simplicius corresponded to three kinds of causes. The first is what Charles called 'a particular activating cause'.[9] It is a body in a certain condition (*sôma pôs echon*), or a body in a certain condition according to a differentia (*sôma echomenon kata diaphoran*, 2.390). In (3) we seem to have a distinction between the practical impulse and the rational impulse. What Simplicius calls 'an individual impulse' is the practical impulse. Simplicius distinguishes between 'functioning from an individual impulse' and 'functioning from a rational impulse'. The latter is specified by 'acting in accordance with virtue'. 'Acting according to virtue' is acting from a rational impulse. The predicate, as an activity, may also be described as 'acting from a rational impulse'.

In several passages in Simplicius, however, the predicate is said to 'participate in' the quality:

> Yet the qualities that are real according to some primary cause are so far from being correlated with the predicates that they themselves produce the real predicates, as, for example, *phronêsis* (practical wisdom) produces *to phronein* (thinking wisely), either through activity or through being participated in *êtoi kat' energeian ê en tôi metechesthai, In Cat.* p. 216,27-31).

The word *metechesthai* is used as a passive infinitive, and should be translated 'being participated in'. That which participates in practical wisdom, a permanent

---

[9] D. Charles, *Aristotle's Philosophy of Action* (London and Ithaca, N.Y., 1984) 44. See also J.L. Ackrill, 'Aristotle's distinction between *energeia* and *kinêsis*', in *New Essays on Plato and Aristotle*, ed. R. Bambrough (London, 1965, repr. 1979) 121-41.

disposition of the soul (3.459), is the predicate 'thinking wisely', but this same predicate is that towards which the rational impulse is directed. Practical wisdom, as a corporeal cause, produces the predicate through its own activity (cf. 1.89).

Another passage in Simplicius speaks of the participation of the predicate in the disposition:

> The Stoics called a quality a *hexis* (disposition), but the members of the Academy called them *hekta* (habits), and they said that the term was formed from *to echesthai* (being possessed), just as the *ennoêmata methektika* (the notions that are capable of participating) are formed from *to metechesthai* (being participated in), and the *ptôseis teuktai*[10] (cases that are capable of attaining) from *to tunchanesthai* (being attained, *In Cat.* p. 209,11-12).

Was Simplicius saying that the Stoics used an active term *hexis* (disposition) in spite of the fact that they said that the term was formed from the passive infinitive *to echesthai* (being possessed)? Was he arguing that they acted in a similar fashion when they formed the term *ennoêmata methektika* (notions that are capable of participating), since *methektika* (capable of participating) is active in meaning, but formed from the passive infinitive (*to metechesthai*) and again, when they formed *ptôseis teuktai* (cases that are capable of attaining), since *teuktai* (capable of attaining) is active in meaning but formed from the passive infinitive *to tunchanesthai* (being attained)? If this is the point that Simplicius is making, the specifications in the passage are Stoic. There is a possibility, however, that lines two to the end, beginning with the words 'and they said that the term

---

[10] The word *teuktos* seems to be synonymous with *teuktikos*, a word that appears in Aristotle's *Ethics* with the meaning 'being able to attain' (*E.N.* 1142b22).

was formed from being possessed' describe the Academic position.[11]

Unlike the third class of activity described by Simplicius, the second class does not require a quality or an impulse. The process arises naturally. By nature the seed attracts the matter and shapes the measures in it. The medical powers effect a cure. It is at this point that the Stoic rejection of teleology comes to the fore. The seed is a power even if it never produces a plant or an animal, just as the soul is a power if it lacks the power of sight, or even intelligence. The seed has the power of producing a process or an effect, although this power might be hampered by a defect in its own nature, or by external circumstances. The production of natural processes is an activity of the seminal *logos*, and a function of the world soul.

If the predicate were merely a state of affairs and an activity, it would be of little importance. It is significant because it is causally related to the corporeal body, and because it and the attribute share a common source, the corporeal body.

Zeno says that a cause is that 'because of which'; and that that for which there is a cause is an attribute (*sumbebêkos*). And that the cause is a corporeal body (*sôma*), and that that for which there is a cause is a predicate (*katêgorêma*). But it is impossible that the cause should be present and that that for which there is a cause should not be real ... A cause is that because of which something happens, as, for example, thinking wisely (*to phronein*) arises because of practical wisdom (*phronêsis*) and living (*to zên*) because of soul (*psuchê*), and acting moderately (*to sôphronein*) because of moderation (*sôphrosunê*). For it is impossible, if there is moderation in regard to some things, that there should not be acting moderately, or, if there is soul, that there

[11] Cf. A. Graeser. *Zenon von Kition. Positionen und Probleme* (Berlin, 1975) 74-5.

should not be living, or, if there is practical wisdom, that there should not be thinking wisely (*Ec.* I, p. 138,14-22 = 1.89).[12]

Of the passages that connect the predicate with the attribute, the most important is found in Stobaeus:

> He (sc. Chrysippus) says that only the present is real, but he says that the past and the future subsist, and are not real at all (*Ec.* I, p. 106,18-20 = 2.509).

At this point the reading and translation of the Greek raises problems. I shall, therefore, quote the Greek as it appears in Wachsmuth's edition of Stobaeus (*Ec.* I, p. 106,20-1): *ei mê hôs kai katêgorêmata huparchein legetai mona ta sumbebêkota.*[13] Von Arnim, however, emended the text to read: *phêsin, hôs kai katêgorêmata* (2.509). We may translate Wachsmuth's *ei mê hôs* by 'except that' and von Arnim's *hôs* by 'since'. The clause may be translated as: 'Except that (or since) even predicates are said to be real, that is, only the attributes.'

The passage continues:

> As, for example, 'walking' is real for me when I am walking, but it is not real when I have lain down or am sitting down (2.509).

Lloyd, commenting on this sentence, wrote: 'The present actually belongs, he (sc. Chrysippus) went on, in the sense that verbs are truly attributed – "attributes like walking actually belong to me only when I am walking: when I am lying down or sitting down they do not actually belong" ... He was not referring to the predicate "walking", but the attribute signified by it; for

---

[12] ibid. 82-9.
[13] Diels accepted this reading. See H. Diels, *Doxographi Graeci* (Berlin, 1879, repr. 1976) fr. 26, pp. 461-2.

the predicate would belong in a false proposition.'[14] Chrysippus in this context is considering a particular kind of experience, such that I can say 'this is real for me', as, for example, 'walking when I am walking', 'feeling cold when I am cold', or 'feeling hungry when I am hungry'. All of these are attributes and all of these are predicates.

Also significant is a Stoic definition of a true proposition, preserved by Sextus Empiricus, which was translated by Bury as follows:

> Now as to this definite proposition, 'This man is sitting', or 'This man is walking', they declare that it is true *when the thing predicated, such as 'sitting', or 'walking', belongs to the object indicated* (*hotan tôi hupo tên deixin piptonti sumbebêkêi to katêgorêma, Math.* 8.100 = 2.205).[15]

I would suggest as a possible translation for the part of the sentence in italics 'when the predicate, such as "sitting" or "walking", is the attribute (*sumbebêkos*) of the object of reference.' What actually belongs is not the predicate but the attribute.

The predicates and the attributes occur together in a diaeresis in Philo:

> And again, of the incorporeals some are complete and others are incomplete ... Again, of the incomplete the diaereseis which are related to what are called predicates

[14] A.C. Lloyd, 'Activity and description in Aristotle and the Stoa', *Dawes Hicks Lecture on Philosophy. Proceedings of the British Academy* (1970) 8-9. See also G. Watson, *The Stoic Theory of Knowledge* (Belfast, 1966) 40; A.A. Long, 'Language and thought in Stoicism', in *Problems in Stoicism*, ed. A.A. Long (London, 1971) 89; G. Kerferd, 'The problem of *synkatathesis* and *katalepsis* in Stoic Doctrine', in *Les stoïciens et leur logique*, ed. J. Brunschwig (Paris, 1978) 267.

[15] R.G. Bury, *Sextus Empiricus*, 11 (Loeb, 1967).

and attributes and whatever are under these are closely connected (2.182).[16]

Galen, however, is probably correct in saying that the attributes are corporeal (2.377).[17] The Stoics seem to have held that even negative predicates corresponded to attributes. Alexander of Aphrodisias refers to adversaries who argued that the proposition 'Dion is not walking' is affirmative. They held that the proposition did not deny that 'there is a Dion, who is such that the proposition "This man does not walk" can be considered an affirmation about him'.[18] Similarly, we find in Apuleius a statement to the effect that the proposition 'Pleasure is not good' is affirmative (2.204a).

The Stoics recognized definite pronouns which included the personal pronouns (e.g. I, you), and the

---

[16] Schmidt and Barwick argued that a passage in a Scholiast on Dionysius Thrax, which has as its subject the *idia* (essential characteristics) and the *parepomena*, was based on Stoic teachings. Barwick held that the latter was used by later Stoics in place of the term *sumbebêkota* (attributes). See K. Barwick, 'Probleme der Stoischen Sprachtheorie und Rhetorik', Abh. der Sächs. Akad. Wiss. Leipzig Phil.-hist. Kl. 49, 3 (1957) 47; R. Schmidt, *Stoicorum Grammatica* (Halle, 1839) 43-4; R.T. Schmidt, *Die Grammatik der Stoiker. Einführung, Übersetzung und Bearbeitung* von K. Hülser (Wiesbaden, 1979) 67-8.

[17] The Stoic *sumbebêkos* (attribute) was either Aritostelian in origin or shared a common source in the Academy with the Aristotelian term. Aristotle defined the term in *Topics* 102b4-10. For the Aristotelian attribute see É. de Strycker, 'Concepts-clés et terminologie dans les livres ii à vii des Topiques', in *Aristotle on Dialectic. The Topics*, ed. G.E.L. Owen (Oxford, 1968) 146-8; G. Verbeke, 'La notion de propriété dans les topiques', in *Aristotle on Dialectic*, 262-3; H.J. Krämer, *Platonismus und Hellenistische Philosophie* (Berlin, 1971) 93, n. 368. The crucial passage for Epicurus' use of the term is *Ep.* 1.68-69,4. For a discussion of the term see H. Steckel, *Epikurs Prinzip der Einheit von Schmerzlosigkeit und Lust* (Göttingen, 1960) 70-3; P. Natorp, *Forschungen zur Geschichte des Erkenntnisproblems im Altertum* (Berlin, 1884) 230; E. Asmis, *Epicurus' Scientific Method* (Ithaca, N.Y., 1984) 250 and n. 20.

[18] Alex. Aphr. *Comm. in Anal. Pr.* p. 402,11-12 Wallies.

demonstrative pronouns (e.g. this, that),[19] and indefinite pronouns (e.g. someone, anyone). These pronouns determined the truth value of three types of propositions. An indefinite proposition (e.g. 'Someone is sitting') is true when the definite (e.g. 'This man is sitting') is found to be true (2.205). Again, if an intermediate proposition is true (e.g. 'Socrates is sitting') the corresponding definite proposition ('This man is sitting') must be true.

If the statement 'This man is wise' is true, we must be able to say that *to phronein* (being wise) is an attribute which has as its cause the *phronêsis* (practical wisdom) which is present in this man. In this case, the term *houtos* (this man) is an object of reference. We must also be able to say that *to phronein* is a predicate whose cause is the *phronesis* in this man. Here, the word *houtos* is a case (*ptôsis*). Since the Stoics connected an activity, such as walking, with the soul,[20] we may say that, if 'This man is walking' is true, *to peripatein* (walking) must be an attribute which has as its cause the soul in this man, and a predicate which has the same cause.

For further evidence regarding the nature of the predicate, I shall turn to two passages which shed a good deal of light on the Stoic *lekton*. The word *lekton* should be translated as 'that which can be spoken' or 'the expressible'. The term was used to describe the predicate (*SVF* 3.8, Archedemus) and the case (2.166).

A *lekton* is that which subsists according to a rational presentation (*lekton de huparchein phasi to kata logikên phantasian*), and a rational presentation is that according

---

[19] For the definite pronouns see M. Pohlenz, 'Die Begründung der abendländischen Sprachlehre durch die Stoa', *Nach. Ges. Wiss. Göttingen Phil.-hist. Kl.* 3, 6 (1939) 164; A.C. Lloyd, 'Grammar and metaphysics in the Stoa', in *Problems in Stoicism*, 67-8 and 73, n. 36; H. Hagius, *The Stoic Theory of the Parts of Speech* (Ph.D. diss. Columbia University, 1979) 160-7.

[20] Cleanthes defined 'walking' as a breath let down from the ruling part of the soul to the feet, and Chrysippus as the ruling part of the soul itself (2.836).

to which it is possible to express by a *logos* that which has been presented (2.187 cf. 2.181).

The distinction which the Stoics may have made between *huparchein* and *huphistanai* has occasioned some lively discussion in recent years.[21] Goldschmidt concluded that both verbs carry the idea of existence, reinforced in the case of *huparchein* by the notion of actuality.[22] Whatever concept of existence we attach to the *lekton*, it must be consistent with the nature of the *lekton* as an incorporeal (2.331), and its dependence upon the corporeal presentation.

Mates,[23] W. and M. Kneale,[24] and Long[25] translated the word *logos* in the second half of this sentence as 'discourse'. Kerferd has incorrectly, I believe, argued in favour of 'reason'.[26] 'To express by a *logos* (*logôi parastêsai*)[27] that which has been presented' is 'to utter articulate sound, capable of signifying the state of affairs that is being conceived (*tou nooumenou pragmatos*)' (2.167). The common and the proper name, both parts of the *logos* (3.22), signified a quality. The verb (*rhêma*), a third part of the *logos*, signified an uncompounded predicate (3.22). The *logos*, which had as its parts the

---

[21] See H. Dörrie, '*Hupostasis*. Wort- und Bedeutungsgeschichte', *Nach. Akad. Wiss. Göttingen Phil.-hist. Kl.* 1, 3 (1955) 35-92; A.C. Lloyd, 'Activity and Description in Aristotle and the Stoa', *Dawes Hicks Lecture on Philosophy. Proceedings of the British Academy* 56 (1971) 1-16; P. Hadot, 'Zur Vorgeschichte des Begriffs "Existenz" *Huparchein* bei den Stoikern', *Arch. f. Begriffsgeschichte* 13 (1969) 115-27; V. Goldschmidt, '*Huparchein Huphistanai* dans la philosophie stoicienne', *REG* 85 (1972) 331-44.

[22] Goldschmidt (1972) 344.

[23] B. Mates, *Stoic Logic*[2] (California, 1961) 15.

[24] W. and M. Kneale, *The Development of Logic* (Oxford, 1962) 140.

[25] Long (1971) 82-3.

[26] Kerferd (1978) 253-4.

[27] G. Cortassa, 'Pensiero e linguaggio nella teoria Stoica del *lekton*', *Rivista di Filologia e Istruzione Classica* 106 (1978) 389, translates this phrase as 'esporre (esprimere) con un' espressione significante'. See also A.-J. Voelke, 'Représentation, signification et communication dans le stoïcisme', *Actes du XVIIIe Congrès des sociétés de philosophie de langue française* (Strasbourg, July 1980) 346-7.

common noun and the proper name, and the verb, was called the *logos* capable of uttering (*logos prophorikos*).
This conclusion is supported by a passage in Diogenes Laertius:

> The presentation leads the way, then the intelligence that is capable of expression (*dianoia eklalêtikê*) expresses through *logos* what it has experienced as the result of the presentation (2.52).

Pasquino interpreted three of the incorporeals convincingly when he wrote: 'Lieu, temps et vide (pour le monde dans le moment de l'*ekpurôsis*) sont les conditions de possibilité des événements produits par les corps-causes.'[28] If the *lekton* is interpreted in this way, it is the condition that makes it possible for the *logos* (capable of uttering) to signify the state of affairs that is being conceived, that is, the predicate and the case.

There is no doubt that the *lekton* was regarded as a *noêton* (intelligible). Speaking is defined as uttering articulate sound, capable of signifying the state of affairs that is being conceived (*tou nooumenou pragmatos*, 2.167). The state of affairs is, of course, the incomplete *lekton*, a predicate. Diogenes Laertius wrote that things were conceived by a transition, as, for example, the *lekta* and place (7.53 = 2.87). Sextus Empiricus defined the proposition as an intelligible (2.195). Since the proposition was composed of a case and a predicate (Plut. *Quaest. Plat.* 1009C), presumably both of these were intelligibles.

Whether we should regard the *lekta* as thoughts is an open question. The evidence in Simplicius is conflicting. In one passage he writes that 'what is said and *lekta* are thoughts' (*In Cat.* p. 10,3-4); in another he refers to

---

[28] P. Pasquino, 'Le statut ontologique des incorporels dans l'ancien stoicisme', in *Les stoïciens et leur logique*, 383. For the incorporeals see also E. Bréhier, *La théorie des incorporels dans l'ancien stoïcisme* (Paris, 1962).

'premises ... in thoughts or in the incorporeal *lekta* that subsist according to them (*eite en tois dianoêmasin eite en tois paruphistamenois asômatois lektois*)' (*In Cat.* p. 397,8-14). It seems better to assume that the rational presentation was the 'thought' and that the *lekton* was an intelligible that subsisted according to this thought.[29]

The *lekta* may be specified by either statements (*katêgoriai*) or propositions (*axiômata*). The proposition, e.g. 'It is day', has a contradictory: 'Not: it is day' (S.E. *Math.* 8.89 cf. D.L. 7.69). The statement has a contrary: 'It is not day.' The proposition receives assent from the impulse; the statement specifies the presentation.

Since the predicate and the case composed the proposition, I shall say a few words about the Stoic 'case', and mention briefly Diogenes Laertius' definition of the proposition. A case, such as the word 'Dion', is a *pragma* (state of affairs) and a *lekton* (S.E. *Math.* 8.11-12 = 2.166, cf. 2.164). The case was signified by articulate sound. We are told that the articulate sound 'dog' signified a case under which falls the barking animal, the marine animal, the philosopher and the star (S.E. *Math.* 11.28-9). Here the word 'case' serves as the first term of a diaeresis of homonyms. Dionysius Thrax states specifically that 'the five cases belong to the class of that which is signified, not to that of articulate sound'.[30]

Diogenes Laertius' definition of the proposition is extremely difficult to interpret:

[29] See Long (1971) 80-1. In his *Commentary on Aristotle's Prior Analytics*, Ammonius states that thoughts are distinguished from *lekta* (68,5-7). In his *Commentary on the De Interpretatione*, moreover, we find a statement to the effect that the *lekton* is intermediate between the thought and the *pragma* (17,24-8). These statements are of little significance, however, because he equated the *pragmata* with the *tunchanonta* (things, *In Analyt. Pr.* 68,4-5).

[30] For a discussion of 'case' see P. Hadot, 'La notion de "cas" dans la logique stoïcienne', *Le langage. Actes du XIIIᵉ congrès des sociétés de philosophie de langue française* (Neuchâtel, 1966) 109-12. See also Rieth (1933) 173-5; Pohlenz (1939) 168-76; Graeser (1975) 74; R. Pfeiffer, *History of Classical Scholarship* (Oxford, 1968) 244; G. Nuchelmans, *Theories of the Proposition* (Amsterdam, 1973) 72-4.

A proposition is that which is true or false or a state of affairs (*pragma*) complete, such that it can be contradicted (*apophanton*), as Chrysippus says in his *Definitions of Dialectic*: 'a proposition is such that it can be contradicted (*to apophanton*) or affirmed (*ê kataphanton*), for example, "It is day", "Dion walks". The proposition has received its name from "being thought worthy" or "being refused assent" (*ê atheteisthai*, D.L. 7.65).'

In my translation I have used the punctuation adopted by Bochenski.[31] We might, however, put a period after *'Definitions of Dialectic'*. In that case, the sentence which begins 'A proposition is such that it can be contradicted' would not be a quotation from Chrysippus, although the opening sentence in the paragraph might well be attributed to him.

The punctuation is not the only problem we face when we attempt to interpret this passage. Following Bochenski, I translated the word *apophanton* as 'such that it can be contradicted'. Frede, however, argued that it should be translated as 'was behauptet bzw. ausgesagt werden kann' (what can be affirmed, i.e. asserted),[32] and Long as 'that which can be stated'.[33] Since, however, the verb *kataphainein* in Pindar *Nemean* 10.11, seems to mean 'klar werden lassen' (make clear) or 'bestätigen' (confirm), Frede concluded that the words *apophanton* and *kataphanton* were identical in meaning, and suggested that both *apophanton ê* and *ê atheteisthai* were a gloss.[34] Frede, therefore, would write for the lines that we are discussing: 'a proposition is such that it can be affirmed, for example, "It is day", "Dion walks". The

---

[31] J.M. Bochenski, *Formale Logik* (Freiburg, 1956, 1962) 128-9.

[32] M. Frede, *Die Stoische Logik* (Göttingen, 1974) 34.

[33] A.A. Long, 'The Stoic distinction between truth (*hê alêtheia*) and the true (*to alêthes*)', in *Les stoïciens et leur logique*, 301. See also M. Hossenfelder, 'Zur Stoischen Definition von Axioma', *Arch. f. Begriffsgeschichte* 11 (1967) 238-41.

[34] Frede (1974) 38-40.

proposition has received its name from "being thought worthy".'

If we keep the verb *atheteisthai*, and translate it as 'being refused assent' (cf. Polyb. 12.14.6) in the last line of the quotation, we must assume that either *apophanton* or *kataphanton* has a negative connotation. It seems possible that *kataphanton* meant 'such that it can be spoken against'. The prefix *kata* is frequently used in a legal sense to express hostile intent. For instance, the judges are said to give a verdict against (*kata*).[35] Although the evidence is admittedly very tenuous, I would prefer to keep the reading in Diogenes Laertius and translate the sentence as: 'a proposition is such that it can be stated, or contradicted.'[36] My new translation would then read:

> A proposition is that which is true or false or a state of affairs (*pragma*) complete, such that it can be stated, as Chrysippus says in his *Definitions of Dialectic*. A proposition is such that it can be stated or contradicted, for example, 'It is day', 'Dion walks'. The proposition has received its name from 'being thought worthy' or 'being refused assent' (D.L. 7.65).

In this chapter I have considered the predicate from five points of view, as a state of affairs (*pragma*), as an activity, as the effect of a corporeal cause, a disposition of the soul, as a *lekton*, and as a component part of the proposition. The predicate was the connecting link between its source, a disposition of the soul, and the ruling part of the soul which produced the rational presentation according to which it subsisted, and the predicate bridged the gap between the thought process and articulate sound. The Stoics found in the predicate a central, unifying factor for their very complex epistemological system.

---

35 Aesch. *Seven against Thebes* 198, Soph. *Ajax* 449.
36 For further discussion of the 'proposition' see Graeser (1975) 24, n. 2.

4

The Stoic Theory of the Presentation

The word *phantasia* (presentation) has a long history in Plato and Aristotle. Lycos defined the word as 'the state or capacity in virtue of which we say we are appeared to in such and such a way'.[1] For Plato *phantasia* was 'belief brought about through perception' (*Sophist* 264A) and 'a blending of belief and perception' (264B).[2] The Stoics, however, classified belief (*doxa*) as 'assent'. Since the Stoic *phantasia* by its very nature was such that it either received assent, was refused assent, or was denied assent through suspension of judgment, it cannot be conceived as existing at any time apart from the judgment which is implicit in the giving or withholding of assent.

Zeno regarded the *phantasia* as an impression (*tupôsis*) in the soul comparable to the impression made by a signet ring in wax (2.53). Chrysippus is said to have rejected the theory on the grounds that, when a triangle and a quadrangle are perceived at the same time, the soul's *pneuma* must bear the impress of both at the same time (2.56). He held that the presentation was an alteration (*heteroiôsis*) of the soul (2.56). In an 'impression' the soul is the recipient of blows from

---

[1] K. Lycos, 'Aristotle and Plato on "appearing" ', *Mind* 73 (1964) 496.

[2] Cf. *Tim.* 52A7, *Phil.* 39B-C. For *phantasia* in Aristotle see M. Schofield, 'Aristotle on the imagination', in *Aristotle on Mind and the Senses*, ed. G.E.R. Lloyd, G.E.L. Owen (Cambridge, 1978) 99-140; F.H. Sandbach, *Aristotle and the Stoics*, *Cambridge Philological Society* Suppl. 10 (1985) 21-3.

something external to it. In an 'alteration' the soul is itself the cause of the alteration which occurs in the presence of the sense object.[3] If the soul is altered, it has a different configuration at different points in time.

The presentations may be classified as perceptive (*aisthêtikai*), rational (*logikai*), apprehensive (*kataléptikai*) and hormetic (presentations capable of moving an impulse: *hormêtikai*). Aetius, using Chrysippus as his source, defines the presentation as follows:

> A presentation is an affection (*pathos*) arising in the soul, being revealed in itself and revealing that which has produced it. As, for example, when we observe 'the white' through sight, there is an affection which has arisen through sight in the soul. And <according to> this affection we are able to say that something white underlies and moves us (2.54).[4]

At first glance, this definition of the presentation seems to refer to the apprehensive presentation. In fact, 'white' was used as a specification for this apprehension (2.84). It seems better, however, to assume that the definition is what it claims to be, a definition which applies to every kind of presentation.

The manner in which the presentations were formed is described clearly by Diogenes Laertius:

> Of the presentations, according to them (sc. the Stoics) some are perceptive (*aisthêtikai*), others are not. Perceptive are those that are apprehended through a sense organ (*aisthêtêrion*) or sense organs, not perceptive

[3] For 'alteration' see J.W. Stannard, *The Psychology of the Passions in the Old Stoa* (Illinois, 1958) 111-12, 258-9, nn. 444, 446, 447.

[4] A statement attributed to Carneades is similar (Sextus Empiricus, *Math.* 7.161-2). For Carneades see C.L. Stough, *Greek Skepticism* (California, 1969); B. Wiesniewski, *Karneades. Fragmente. Text und Kommentar* (Warsaw, 1970); G. Striker, 'Sceptical strategies', in *Doubt and Dogmatism. Studies in Hellenistic Epistemology*, ed. M. Schofield, M. Burnyeat, J. Barnes (Oxford, 1980) 54-83.

are those that are apprehended through the thinking process (*dianoia*), as, for example, the incorporeals and the other things that are apprehended by *logos*. Of the perceptive <some> arise from those things that are real (*ta huparchonta*) with yielding and assent. Those of the presentations that arise as if they were from those things that are real are impressions (*emphaseis*, 2.61).

The noun *aisthêtêrion* (sense organ) shows Aristotelian influence. Since it is never listed as a part of the Stoic soul, it seems better to assume that the 'thinking process', which is identical with the ruling part of the soul, apprehended the perceptive presentation through the perception. A passage in Aetius states that the ruling part of the soul produced the perceptions (2.836). What Diogenes Laertius calls 'impressions' seems to be the same as Sextus Empiricus' 'false presentations', specified by 'The oar in the water is broken' (2.65). Perceptive presentations that arise from those things that are real are, of course, apprehensive presentations.

The apprehension of the presentation is followed by an act of assent to the same presentation, or by the withholding of assent. The giving of assent is a separate act, distinguishable from the presentation, although it may occur simultaneously with it (3.177).

The Stoics also classified presentations as plausible, implausible, plausible and implausible, and neither plausible nor implausible. They divided the plausible again into true, false, true and false, and neither true nor false, and classified some of the true presentations as apprehensive (S.E. *Math*. 7.242-7 = 2.65). In his definition of a true presentation Sextus Empiricus writes: 'True are those of which it is possible to make a true statement (*katêgoria*), as, for example, "It is day", when day is present, or "It is light" ' (*Math*. 7.244 = 2.65). He also writes that 'some of the perceptibles and some of the intelligibles are true, the perceptibles not directly but with reference to the intelligibles that correspond to them' (*Math.* 8.10 = 2.195). The incorporeal proposition is an intelligible (*Math.* 9.10 = 2.195).[5] True presentations may be perceptive or rational. The statement 'Twice two is four' should probably be regarded as a true, rational presentation, rather than a *doxa* (3.172).[6]

The Stoics defined the false presentations as 'those of which it is possible to make a false statement,[7] as, for example, that the oar in the water is broken, or that the stoa is foreshortened' (*Math.* 7.244 = 2.65). If this presentation reveals itself and that which has caused it, it reveals an impression, for example, the reflection of light on the water. Because it does not reveal the corporeal body and its attribute, it is false, and it is false whether it is recognized as such or not. The giving of assent to such a presentation is an error in judgment. Assent to a false presentation is made by a *doxa*. I may, of course, grasp the oar without giving assent to the false presentation that it is broken. Assent to the false presentation was not a necessary condition for the movement of the practical impulse. This is what Chrysippus meant when he wrote:

'Again,' Chrysippus says, 'God makes false presentations and the wise man too, requiring us not to assent or yield to them, but only to act and direct our impulse towards the phenomenon, but we in our folly because of our weakness give assent to such presentations' (3.177, cf. 2.994).

[5] Chrysippus, however, is quoted as saying that 'the generic "sweet" is intelligible, but that that which is a species and a fresh experience is a perceptible' (2.81). The 'intelligible' in this case would appear to be a concept (*ennoia*).

[6] See p. 121.

[7] Kerferd translated this sentence as 'False are those (sc. presentations) from which it is possible to constitute a false predicate'. G.B. Kerferd, 'The problem of *synkatathesis* and *katalepsis* in Stoic doctrine', in *Les stoïciens et leur logique*, ed. J. Brunschwig (Paris, 1978) 263.

If the true and false presentation, 'Electra is a Fury', reveals itself and that which has caused it, it reveals the corporeal body, Electra, and the attribute 'being real', but it also reveals the hallucination 'being a Fury':

> True and false, as, for example, the one (sc. presentation) that fell upon Orestes in his madness which had its source in Electra (for inasmuch as it came from some *huparchon* (that which is real) it was true, for Electra was real; but inasmuch as it came from a Fury, it was false, for she was not a Fury) (*Math*. 7.244-5 = 2.65).

This true and false presentation may be specified by two statements: 'Electra is real', and 'Electra is a Fury'. One predicate is described as true; the other as false. We should recall that Sextus Empiricus wrote: 'They (sc. the Stoics) say that it (sc. a proposition) is true when the predicate is the attribute of the object of reference' (*Math*. 8.100 = 2.205). The predicate 'is a Fury' is not an attribute of Electra. How, then, does this predicate differ in kind from the predicate 'is broken' in the false statement 'The oar in the water is broken'? Is it not possible to define this false presentation 'The oar in the water is broken' by two statements: 'The oar is real' and 'The oar is broken'? We must look for an answer to these questions by examining the nature of the two statements.

'The oar in the water is broken' is an impossible proposition. This kind of proposition was defined by Diogenes Laertius as: 'The impossible is that which does not admit of being true, as, for example, "The earth is flying" ' (7.75); and by Boethius as: 'The impossible is that which never admits of any truth since other things outside prevent the realization of it.'[8] The object of reference for an attribute which cannot and will never exist is itself non-existent. 'Electra is a Fury', on the

---

[8] Boethius, *Comm. In Arist. De Interp.* 235.1-3.

other hand, is a non-necessary proposition. This was
defined by Diogenes Laertius in the words: 'The
non-necessary is that which is both true and capable of
being false if external circumstances do not prevent it, as,
for example, "Dion walks" ' (7.75 = 2.201).[9] 'Being a Fury'
is a non-necessary attribute of Electra, and the absence
of this attribute does not preclude its presence at another
time. Neither the presence nor the absence of this
attribute destroys the 'reality' of Electra.

Since the concept (*ennoia*) and the anticipation
(*prolêpsis*) seem to have formed the content of the
rational presentation, it is appropriate at this point in
the discussion to consider how these terms were formed.
The evidence for man's intellectual development from the
time of his birth is found in Aetius:[10]

> The Stoics say: When a man is born, he has the ruling
> part of his soul like a papyrus serviceable for writing. On
> this he inscribes each one of his concepts. That kind of
> inscribing which arises through sensations (*aisthêseis*) is
> first. For perceiving something, as, for example, white,
> they have a memory of it, after it has disappeared. But
> when many memories of the same kind arise, then we say
> that we have experience; for experience is a number of
> presentations of the same kind.
>
> Of the concepts some arise naturally in the ways
> mentioned above, and undesignedly, others through some
> instruction and diligence; the latter are called concepts

---

[9] For the Stoic impossible and non-necessary propositions see M.E. Reesor,
'Fate and Possibility in Early Stoic Philosophy', *Phoenix* 19 (1965) 292-5.

[10] Diels argued in his *Doxographi Graeci* that, since identical passages occur
in Plutarch's *De Placitis Epitome* and Stobaeus' *Eclogae* 1, both authors must
have been using a common source, the *De Placitis* of Aetius, an unknown
writer who lived in the first century BC. From these passages, Diels held, we
are able to reconstruct the lost works of Aetius. See H. Diels, *Doxographi
Graeci*[4] (Berlin, 1879, repr. 1976). Aetius refers to specific Stoics in the *De
Placitis*, e.g. Zeno, Chrysippus and Posidonius, and to the Stoics in general.
Passages that are attributed to 'the Stoics' do not show any consistency in
interpretation.

(*ennoiai*) only, the former are also anticipations (*prolêp-seis, Plac.* IV.11.1-5 = 2.83).[11]

In this passage the anticipations are described as a special kind of concept. They are those that arise naturally through sensation and experience.

Sandbach believed that part of the passage in Aetius had fallen out and that there was a lacuna between paragraphs one and two of this passage. He argued that the missing section could be reconstructed from a passage in Diogenes Laertius:

> Of those things that are conceived some have been conceived by direct experience, some by resemblance, some by analogy, some by transposition, some by composition, and some by contrariety. By direct experience the perceptibles (*aisthêta*) are conceived (*enoêthê*) ... Some things are conceived by a transition, as, for example, the expressibles (*lekta*) and place. Something just and good is conceived naturally (2.87).[12]

In this paragraph, Diogenes writes: 'By direct experience the perceptibles are conceived.' We may recall that experience was preceded by perception and memory, and that the anticipation arises naturally through memory and experience. When the perceptibles are conceived as intelligibles, they are presumably conceived as anticipations. Similarly, when Diogenes writes: 'Something just and good is conceived naturally', we may interpret the sentence as meaning: 'Something just and good is conceived as an intelligible, that is, as an anticipation.'

[11] For a discussion of this passage see M. Pohlenz, 'Grundfragen der stoischen Philosophie', *Abh. Ges. Wiss. Göttingen, Phil.-hist. Kl.* 3, 26 (1940) 82-7; F.H. Sandbach, '*Ennoia* and *prolêpsis* in the Stoic theory of knowledge', in *Problems in Stoicism*, ed. A.A. Long (London, 1971) 25-6.

[12] For this passage see C. Imbert, 'Stoic logic and Alexandrian poetics', in *Doubt and Dogmatism* (1980) 190; I. Mueller, 'Geometry and scepticism', in *Science and Speculation*, ed. J. Barnes, *et al.* (Cambridge, 1982) 78.

It is not very likely that the passage in Aetius represents the views of Chrysippus. Chrysippus regarded the concepts and anticipations as parts of a *logos*, and there is no suggestion that one could be defined in terms of the other (De Lacy, V.3.2). The perception and the anticipation were one of his many criteria of truth (2.105), not the perception and concept.

In the passage quoted above, Aetius defined the notion (*ennoêma*) as follows: 'A notion is an impression of the mind of a rational animal. When the impression falls upon a rational soul, it is called a notion, having received its name from the intellect' (2.83) Diogenes Laertius similarly defines the notion as an impression of the mind and specifies the term by 'the likeness of a horse, which arises even if the horse is not present' (1.65). The use of the term 'impression' (*phantasma*) in these passages cannot be reconciled with the definition of the term in another passage in Aetius, a passage which appears to be based on Chrysippus (*Plac.* IV. 12. 5 = 2.54):

> An impression is that to which we are drawn by the empty, appearance-producing fancy; these arise in those who are melancholy and mad. The tragic character, Orestes, when he says ... speaks these words as one who is mad, for he sees nothing, but only supposes that he does.

The act of thinking was distinguished from the concept: 'Since we have memories of things that are perceived by the senses, whenever we set these in motion, they are to be called by the term *noêsis* (act of thinking); but whenever they happen to be silent, they are called *ennoiai* (concepts).'[13] The act of thinking arises from an *aisthêsis* (sensation or perception), or not without an *aisthêsis* (2.88).

[13] Galen, *Inst. Log.* p. 7,22-8,7. See B. Mates, *Stoic Logic*[2] (California, 1961) 12-13.

Certainly, what came to be known as the *logos endiathetos* (*logos* residing in the fixed disposition of the soul) must have had much the same function as the *noêsis*. Unfortunately, we know very little about this term. The '*logos* residing in the fixed disposition' is described as 'the choice of what is akin, and the avoidance of what is alien, the knowledge of skills pertaining to this, the laying hold (*antilêpsis*) of the virtues according to one's own nature, and those things related to the emotions'.[14] In the introduction to Plutarch's *Epitome* IV.11 we read: 'How arise the perception, the concept and the *logos* according to the fixed disposition (*ho kata endiathesin logos*).' The word *diathesin* appears in the manuscripts and was emended to *endiathesin* by Wyttenbach. The emendation was accepted by Diels (*Dox. Gr.* 400). From its association with perception and the concept in Plutarch's *Epitome*, Mühl argued that 'the *logos* residing in the fixed disposition' was passive.[15] The terms for perception and concept, however, can be active as well as passive. Pohlenz was probably right in accepting Nemesius' statement that 'the *logos* residing in the fixed disposition' is 'the movement arising in the rational part'.[16]

The function of the thinking process, however, was not

[14] Sextus Empiricus, *Pyrrh. Hyp.* 1.65.

[15] M. Mühl, 'Der *logos endiathetos* und *prophorikos* von der älteren Stoa bis zur Synode von Sirmium 351', *Arch. f. Begriffsgeschichte* 7 (1962) 12.

[16] M. Pohlenz, 'Die Begründung der abendländischen Sprachlehre durch die Stoa', *Nach. Ges. Wiss. Göttingen Phil.-hist. Kl. 3*, 6 (1939) 193-4.

Mühl believed that the distinction between 'the *logos* residing in the fixed disposition' and 'the *logos* capable of expressing' originated in a discussion between the Academy and the Old Stoa regarding the *logos* of animals in the time of Zeno (10-11). He drew attention to the attack on animal sacrifice in Theophrastus' *Concerning Piety*. (See W. Pötscher, *Theophrastus Peri Eusebeias* (Leiden, 1964). Pohlenz held that the distinction was made in the time of Carneades (214-129 BC), a contemporary of Diogenes of Babylon, and that it arose in a dispute between the Academy and the Stoics regarding the essential difference between men and animals (192-7). He based his conclusions on two passages in Sextus Empiricus (*Math.* 8.173-5, and *Pyrrh. Hyp.* 1.62-3), and a passage in Porphyry's *De Abstinentia* (3.2).

merely to form concepts and anticipations from sensa-
tions and perceptions, but to exercise the poetic
imagination and indulge in fantasies and dream
imagery. Fantasies and hallucinations were rational
presentations, which were probably regarded as false, or
true and false presentations. Since the Stoics attached a
great deal of importance to dreams, dream imagery must
have been interpretated as a true, or a true and false
presentation. Great poems, such as those of Homer,
presented the truth, and their meaning could be
determined allegorically. Chrysippus, for instance,
argued that Athena's leap from the head of Zeus signified
the emanation of the voice from the head (2.909).
Posidonius, moreover, defined poetry (*poiêsis*) as a poetic
creation (*poiêma*), capable of signifying, containing an
imitation of things divine and human.[17] How, then, did
the poet arrive at these truths? Through the imaginative,
creative powers of the ruling part of the soul, he formed
true presentations and true and false presentations that
reached far beyond sense data to ultimate truth.[18]

---

[17] D.L. 7.60 = Theiler 1 (1982) F 458, II (1982) 400-1. See also P. De Lacy,
'Stoic views of poetry', *AJP* 69 (1948) 241-71; C. Imbert (1980) 182-216.

[18] For the rational presentation see particularly P. Couissin, 'Le stoïcisme de
la nouvelle académie', *Rev. d'histoire de la philosophie* 3 (1929) 242-76,
reprinted in English translation as 'The Stoicism of the New Academy', in *The
Skeptical Tradition*, ed. M. Burnyeat (California, 1983) 31-63; C. Imbert,
'Théorie de la représentation et doctrine logique dans le stoïcisme ancien', in
Les stoïciens et leur logique, 223-49; Imbert (1980) 182-216; M. Frede, 'Stoics
and Skeptics on clear and distinct impressions', in *The Skeptical Tradition*,
65-93.

5

The Apprehension and the
Apprehensive Presentation

My discussion of the Stoic apprehension (*katalêpsis*) will begin with a story told about Zeno in Cicero's *Prior Academics* (11,145 = 1.66):

> For, when he had pointed to his hand with his fingers extended, he said: 'Presentation (*phantasia*) is of this kind.' Then, when he had contracted his fingers a little, 'Assent (*sunkatathesis*) is of this kind'.[1] Then, when he had brought them together and made a fist, he said that this was apprehension (*katalêpsis*); from this comparison he gave to that the name of *katalêpsis* which had not existed before. But when he had moved his left hand to his right hand and squeezed the fist tightly and strongly, he said that exact knowledge (*epistêmê*) was like that, but that no one except the wise man was in possession of it.

The first two kinds of assent were open to all men; the third was exercised by the wise man only. There is no reason to identify the term 'assent' in this passage with *doxa* (belief), or to believe that the wise man did not exercise assent. In fact, Cicero tells us that the wise man

---

[1] The verb *sunkatatithemai* appears only once in Plato, *Gorgias* 501C. Ast translated it by the Latin *assentior*. The noun *sunkatathesis* does not appear at all. In Aristotle the situation is similar. The verb is found in the *Topics* (116a11), and the noun not at all.

on occasion gave assent: 'Particularly, since you your-
selves say that the wise man in a state of rage refrains
from every assent, because no distinction in visible objects
is apparent' (*Ac. Pr.* 11,48 = 3.551). The wise man may
have used 'assent' in the same way as Sphaerus did when
he reached for the pomegranates. When Sphaerus
reached out his hand for the pomegrantes, the king
exclaimed that he had given assent to a false presentation,
but Sphaerus replied that he had given assent not to their
being pomegranates but to its being reasonable to suppose
that they were pomegranates (1.624). Sphaerus in other
words moved his impulse to give assent to the proposition:
'It is reasonable that these are pomegranates.' It is
probable, therefore, that the assent mentioned in the
passage from Zeno was assent to a proposition.

There is no direct connection between the story told
about Zeno and a passage in Sextus Empiricus which
reads:

> For they (sc. the Stoics) say that there are three things
> connected with one another, exact knowledge and belief,
> and that which is set between these, apprehension ...
> They say that exact knowledge is in the wise man only,
> belief in those who are not wise only, but that
> apprehension is common to both, and that this is the
> criterion of truth. Arcesilaus opposed the Stoics who were
> saying this by showing that apprehension is not a
> criterion between exact knowledge and belief (*Math.*
> 7.151-3).[2]

The identification of 'assent' with *doxa* (belief) may have
been made by Arcesilaus.[3] He went on to argue that
apprehension in a wise man is exact knowledge, but in a

---

[2] For a discussion of this passage see A.A. Long, *Hellenistic Philosophy*
(London, 1974) 129; W. Görler, 'Asthenês sunkatathesis, Zur Stoischen
Erkenntnistheorie', *Würzburger Jahrbücher für die Altertumswissenschaft*
N.F. 111 (1977) 83-92.

[3] For Arcesilaus see P. Couissin, 'The Stoicism of the New Academy', in *The
Skeptical Tradition*, ed. M. Burnyeat (California, 1983) 31-51.

man who is not wise belief (ibid.). His criticism seems to be irrelevant. The Stoics would never have acknowledged that apprehension in the man who was not wise was belief. Apprehension was assent to an apprehensive presentation. This definition occurs three times in Sextus Empiricus in passages which deal with Arcesilaus' criticism of Zeno's definition (*Math.* 7.151, 154, 155), and in a later passage in Sextus Empiricus which may likewise be based on Zeno's philosophy (*Math.* 8.397). It is found as well in Alexander of Aphrodisias (2.70). The *doxa*, on the other hand, is assent to the non-apprehensive (3.548). Belief and apprehension were contraries, not, as Arcesilaus objected, belief and exact knowledge.

Arcesilaus raised two further objections: (a) assent is not to a presentation, but to a proposition, (b) no true presentation is found to be of such a kind that it could not be false (*Math.* 7.154). It is clear from the passages that I mentioned above that Zeno used the term 'assent to an apprehensive presentation'. The Stoics, however, may have made some attempt to meet Arcesilaus' objections. They argued, for instance, that the *huparchon*, a proposition, moved the apprehensive presentation (*Math.* 8.85-6), and defined a true presentation as one of which it was possible to make a true statement (*Math.* 7.244 = 2.65).

Exact knowledge (*epistêmê*) was defined as 'a disposition (*hexis*) in the receiving of presentations, made unchangeable by *logos* (*SVF* 1.68, 2.130), or 'a disposition, made unchangeable by *logos*, providing a belief on the basis of presentations, in a manner not blameworthy' (2.93). Other passages, however, define exact knowledge as: (a) an apprehension, reliable and made unchangeable by *logos*, (b) a composite from such apprehensions, (c) a composite of (sc. various) kinds of scientific knowledge (*epistêmai technikai*), possessing stability in itself, such as the virtues have (*Ec.* II, pp.

73,19-74,3). More information is provided by the definitions of a craft (*technê*) as: (a) a composite from apprehensions organized with a view to some end, serviceable for things in life; and (b) a composite organized from apprehensions referring to one end (2.93).[4] It is significant that Sextus Empiricus wrote: 'They say that a craft is a composite of well-organized apprehensions and that the apprehensions arise in the ruling part of the soul' (2.96).

The term 'truth' was also defined as exact knowledge: 'Truth is corporeal, for it is exact knowledge, capable of revealing everything true (*epistêmê pantôn alêthôn apophantikê*)',[5] and exact knowledge is 'the ruling part of the soul in a certain disposition' (*Pyrrh. Hyp.* 2.81-3). The word 'true' was used by the Stoics to describe either propositions or presentations (*Math.* 7.241-52 = 2.65). I would, therefore, translate the Greek in this sentence to mean: 'Exact knowledge, capable of revealing all true (sc. presentations).' Since, however, exact knowledge was either an apprehension or a composite formed from apprehensions, it would reveal only apprehensive presentations. In another passage we read: 'Truth, as exact knowledge, on the contrary, is assumed to be a composite, and an aggregate of several (*pleionôn*)' (*Math.* 7.40-2 = 2.132). The word we should supply with 'several' is, of course, 'apprehensions', *katalêpseôn*).

The Stoic virtues were fixed dispositions of the soul (3.104), or dispositions of the soul (*Ec.* II, p. 73,1-15). The four cardinal virtues, wisdom, justice, courage and

---

[4] For the Stoic 'craft' see E. Grumach, *Physis und Agathon in der alten Stoa. Problemata* 6 (Berlin, 1932) 67-71.

[5] A.A. Long, 'The Stoic distinction between truth (*hê alêtheia*) and the true (*to alêthes*)', in *Les stoïciens et leur logique*, ed. J. Brunschwig (Paris, 1978) 301, translated the word *apophantikê* as 'capable of stating'. For the terms 'truth' and 'true' see also A.A. Long, 'Language and thought in Stoicism', in *Problems in Stoicism*, ed. A.A. Long (London, 1971) 98-101; A. Graeser, *Zenon von Kition. Positionen und Probleme* (Berlin, 1975) 25-30; G.B. Kerferd, 'What does the Wise Man know?' in *The Stoics*, ed. J.M. Rist (California, 1978) 125-36.

temperance, moreover, were exact knowledge and skills.[6] As exact knowledge the cardinal virtue is a composite of corporeal apprehensions,[7] and a disposition of the soul. We have already seen that a cardinal virtue, such as practical wisdom (*phronêsis*) was the corporeal cause of both a predicate (thinking wisely, *to phronein*), and an attribute (thinking wisely, 1.89). If, therefore, virtue is either synonymous with truth, or does not exist independently of it, truth is the corporeal cause of the true predicate. Since both virtue and truth are composites of apprehensions, their identity or inseparability may be assumed. Because of this, the wise man must necessarily speak truthfully. The wise man, however, was capable of making false statements.

There is nothing in either Cicero's or Sextus Empiricus' account to indicate that an apprehension was a perception. According to a passage in Aetius, however, the Stoics held that the perception (*aisthêsis*) was both an assent (*sunkatathesis*) and an apprehension (*katalêpsis*, 2.72), and that all perceptions were true (2.78). How should we interpret these statements? Was every perception an apprehension, or were some perceptions assents but not apprehensions? Was the perception an assent at all? In support of the first premise we may turn to a passage in Galen which reads:

> They say that the statement 'It is possible to see and touch and hear' does not have the same meaning as 'It is possible to perceive by sight, hearing and touch.' For it is possible to see and touch and hear without apprehension (*mê katalêptikôs*), but it is not possible to perceive without apprehension. Such is the interpretation of Simias the Stoic (2.75).

[6] In a Stoic diaeresis in Stobaeus the goods were divided into virtues and those that are not virtues, and virtues, in turn, into those that are exact knowledge and skills (*epistêmai kai technai*), and those that are not (*Ec.* II, p. 58,5-14).

[7] Plutarch states specifically that the virtues and vices are corporeal (2.848).

Further, Cicero states that the wise man can distinguish the false from the true and what cannot be perceived from what can be perceived (2.110). The verb 'to perceive' seems to denote man's capacity for perceiving what is perceived as actually being the way it is perceived to be.

On the other hand, if the perception (*aisthêsis*) which gives assent to the perceptive presentation is an apprehension, then all perceptive presentations, e.g. 'It is day', when day is present, are apprehensive presentations. In his classification of the various kinds of presentations Sextus Empiricus specifically distinguishes perceptive presentations from apprehensive presentations (2.65). It seems better, therefore, to conclude that some perceptions were not apprehensions.

There is, moreover, a passage in Aetius which distinguishes the perception from the assent:

> The Stoics say that the ruling part is the highest part of the soul, that which produces the presentations, assents, perceptions and impulses, and this they call 'reasoning' (2.836).

If the perception was not an assent, it was not an apprehension either. This particular Stoic held that the assent and the perception were produced by the ruling part of the soul, but he did not identify them.

The most significant passage for the possible identification of the perception and the apphension is also in Aetius:

> The Stoics define the *aisthêsis* (perception) in this way. *Aisthêsis* is a 'laying hold' (*antilêpsis*) <through> a sense organ, or an apprehension (*katalêpsis*). The term *aisthêsis* is used in many ways: the disposition (*hexis*), and the power (*dunamis*), and the activity (*energeia*), and the apprehensive presentation arise through a sense organ, and the ruling part itself (*kai auto to hêgemonikon*) <...> from which again sense organs <...> rational *pneumata*

are said to be stretched from the ruling part to the organs (*Dox. Gr.* IV. 8. 1).

Von Arnim emended *kai auto to hêgemonikon* (the ruling part itself) to *kat' auto to hêgemonikon* (according to the ruling part itself), and omitted the lacunae (2.850). The word *antilêpsis* (laying hold) is used to describe *oikeiôsis* (the process by which an animal comes to terms with itself and with its environment) in a passage which reads: 'For *oikeiôsis* seems to be a perception of what belongs and a "laying hold" of it' (1.197).[8] This passage in Aetius should probably not be attributed to the early Stoics. If the perception is a power, the soul has multiple powers. Galen, however, specifically states that there was only one power of the soul in Chrysippus' philosophy (V. 5. 38.9, VII. 1.13). Further, it is not at all clear whether the early Stoics regarded perception as an activity of the soul. It may have been so regarded only when it was recognized as a power. The use of the term 'sense organ' in this passage suggests Aristotelian influence. The early Stoics did not use it.

The main piece of evidence for not identifying the perception and the apprehension is found in Diogenes Laertius:

> The apprehension (*katalêpsis*) arises according to them (sc. the Stoics) by perception (*aisthêsis*) of white, black, rough and smooth, and by reasoning (*logos*) concerning those things that are brought together through demonstration, as, for example, that the gods are and have providence (7.52 = 2.84).

If 'the gods are' and 'the gods have providence' are specifications for the apprehensions, they are also specifications for the apprehensive presentations which

---

[8] *Plutarch's Moralia* XIII, part 2, ed. H. Cherniss (Loeb, Harvard, 1976) 1038C, p. 455, note c.

receive assent from the apprehensions. The apprehension arises 'by perception'; it is not identified with the perception. Similarly, the apprehension arises 'by reasoning' (*logos*), but it itself is not 'reasoning'. The *logos* to which Diogenes is referring is the anticipation (*prolêpsis*), a term which denotes a deep-seated conviction present in all men. The Stoics argued, for instance, that to deny the providence of God was to destroy the anticipation that men have of God. Plutarch writes, 'For God is not only immortal and blessed, but he is preconceived as loving mankind, provident and beneficent.'[9] Chrysippus wrote that the account of goods and evils which he himself introduced and of which he approved was most consistent with life and particularly approached the inborn anticipations (3.69). Using *Adversus Mathematicos* 7.151-3 as evidence, Pohlenz argued that Zeno regarded the apprehension as the criterion of truth.[10] His arguments were successfully refuted by Rieth and Sandbach.[11] Chrysippus in his *Concerning the Logos*, however, stated that the perception (*aisthêsis*) and anticipation (*prolêpsis*) were criteria of truth (2.105). They may have been regarded as criteria because they were the means by which the apprehension arose.

Other terms were regarded as criteria of truth. Chrysippus, Antipater of Tarsus and Apollodorus of Seleucia referred to the apprehensive presentation as the criterion of truth (2.105). Chrysippus is also quoted as saying that the common concepts (*koinai ennoiai*) were the criterion of truth (2.473, p. 154,28-30).[12]

---

[9] Plut. *Comm. Not.* 1075E = 2.1126, cf. *Stoic. Repugn.* 1051E.

[10] M. Pohlenz, 'Zenon and Chrysipp', *Nach. Ges. Wiss. Göttingen* 1 N. F. 2, 9 (1938) 175-81.

[11] O. Rieth, review of Pohlenz, 'Zenon und Chrysipp', *Gnomon* 16 (1940) 105-10; and F.H. Sandbach, '*Phantasia kataleptikê*', in *Problems in Stoicism*, (1971) 15-18.

[12] For the criterion of truth see G. Watson, *The Stoic Theory of Knowledge*

A presentation is defined as an affection arising in the soul, being revealed in itself and revealing that which has produced it (2.54). If the apprehensive presentation is the criterion of truth, it not only reveals that which has caused it but also guarantees that that which has caused it is as it appears to be. The apprehensive presentation is said to be 'capable of apprehending that which underlies accurately, and it receives as its impressions precisely all its particular features (*ta peri autois idiômata*)' (*Math.* 7.248 = 2.65). The apprehension which receives as its impression all these particular features is certainly a perceptive, apprehensive presentation.

I shall argue in Chapter 6 that the minor premise of an argument was a *huparchon*, which moved an apprehensive presentation.[13] This may be specified by arguments such as:

> If there are pleasures, they are indifferents,
> 'This' is a pleasure,
> 'This' (i.e. pleasure) is an indifferent.

and

> If there are appropriate acts, they are reasonably desirable,
> 'This' is an appropriate act,
> 'This' (i.e. appropriate act) is reasonably desirable.

For the apprehensive presentation 'The gods have providence', we may write:

(Belfast, 1966) 34-7; J.M. Rist, *Stoic Philosophy* (Cambridge, 1969) 138-51; Sandbach (1971) 9-21; G. Striker, 'Kriterion *tês alêtheias*', *Nach. Akad. Wiss. Göttingen* 2 (1974) 51-110; Graeser (1975) 56-68; H. von Staden, in his review of A.A. Long, *Problems in Stoicism, AJP* 96 (1975) 232.

[13] See pp. 72-4.

If there are gods, they have providence,
There are gods,
The gods have providence.

I know of no reason why the apprehensive presentations: ' "This" (i.e. pleasure) is an indifferent', ' "This" (i.e. appropriate act) is reasonably desirable', and 'The gods have providence', should be regarded as perceptive presentations, if we disregard the evidence provided by a passage in Plutarch attributed to Chrysippus which reads:

> For only the affections (*pathê*) *are perceptible* (*aisthêta*) *along with their species*, as, for example, pain and fear, and other things of the same kind, but it is possible to perceive theft and adultery and similar things, and, generally, folly and cowardice and other numerous vices, and not only joy and acts of kindness and many other right actions but practical wisdom, courage and the rest of the virtues (*Stoic. Repugn.* 1042E-F = 3.85).

Recently, Burnyeat provided a very ingenious interpretation of the passage. He translated the words that I have italicized from Cherniss' translation by: 'can be perceived along with people's appearance'.[14] He regarded the passage as an example of Stoic physiognomics, and defined the terms as 'a systematic method of inferring mental characteristics in human individuals from bodily features taken as their "signs" '.[15] Zeno and Cleanthes both held that a man's character can be grasped from his appearance (D.L. 7.173).

There is, however, a difference between the presentation 'This man is afraid', and the presentation 'I am afraid'. I may perceive that this man is pale and that his

---

[14] M.F. Burnyeat, 'The origins of non-deductive inference', in *Science and Speculation*, ed. J. Barnes *et al.* (Cambridge, 1982) 229.
[15] ibid. 203.

hands are shaking and infer that he is afraid. My inference, of course, may be wrong, because he may, in fact, have the flu. It is possible, however, to perceive oneself as a thief or a coward in a way in which it is not possible to perceive another individual as being so. One's own state or condition may well be a perceptive presentation or a perceptive, apprehensive presentation. The passage in Plutarch, however, cannot support this view.

If, therefore, the virtues were perceptible, we would have to regard the presentation: 'Virtue is good' as a perceptive, apprehensive presentation. There are now, however, no grounds for regarding the virtues as perceptible. There is every reason to believe that the Stoics recognized rational, apprehensive presentations which received assent from an apprehension (*katalepsis*) by means of the *logos*, or its part, the anticipation.[16]

Although there was no fixed criterion of truth for Chrysippus, the later Stoics accepted the apprehensive presentation as the criterion of truth. In doing so, they may have been influenced by the arguments of Carneades, whose position Sextus Empiricus describes as follows:

> Accordingly, in the affection (*pathos*) of the soul which is based on clarity the criterion must be sought. And this affection ought to be indicative of itself, and of the phenomenon which caused it, and the affection is nothing else than a presentation. Therefore, we must say that a

[16] There is no doubt that Sextus Empiricus believed that the Stoics recognized a rational, apprehensive presentation. He specifically calls 'fifty is few' an apprehensive presentation (*Math*. 7.418). Striker argued, however, that in *Adv. Math*. 7.416-21 Sextus himself and not the older Stoics was responsible for the extension in terminology. She concluded that an apprehensive presentation was a sense impression. Annas adopted the same position. See Striker (above, n. 12) 107-10; J. Annas, 'Truth and knowledge', in *Doubt and Dogmatism*, ed. M. Schofield, M. Burnyeat, J. Barnes (Oxford, 1980) 85. See also the excellent discussion of the apprehensive presentation in A. Bonhöffer, *Epictet und die Stoa* (Stuttgart, 1890, repr. 1968) 228-32.

presentation is an affection of the living creature capable of presenting both itself and the other object (*Math.* 7.161-2).

The early Stoics attached considerable significance to the apprehensive presentation, and, although it was a part of the ruling part of the soul, spoke of it as if it were almost a separate entity. The apprehensive presentation is said to apply pressure and force the assent: 'For it (sc. the apprehensive presentation), being clear and striking, seizes us, almost by the hair, they say, dragging us into assent' (*Math.* 7.257). The apprehension (*katalêpsis*) is not 'in our power' (*eph' hêmin*). Alexander writes in his *Concerning Fate*: 'For they say that "that which is in our power" does not apply in a situation in which we yield when a presentation falls upon us, or when we yield to a presentation that is formed by us ourselves, and feel an impulse towards that which is presented' (2.981).[17]

---

[17] For a discussion of this passage see M.E. Reesor, 'Necessity and fate in Stoic philosophy', in *The Stoics*, ed. J.M. Rist, (California, 1978) 193.

6

That-which-is-real

There has been almost general agreement among scholars that the term *huparchon* (that-which-is-real) in Stoic philosophy means 'exist' when it is applied to material objects and 'to be the case' when it is used to describe propositions. The material object is independent of the act of perceiving and serves to distinguish apprehensive from other presentations.[1]

There is no doubt that the proposition moved an apprehensive presentation:

> For according to them the *huparchon* is true and the contradictory of something, and that which is not a *huparchon* is false and [not] the contradictory of anything. Since it is an incorporeal proposition, it is an intelligible (2.195).[2]

[1] For the *huparchon* and the apprehensive presentation see J.M. Rist, *Stoic Philosophy* (Cambridge, 1969) 137-8; F.H. Sandbach, '*Phantasia kataleptike*', in *Problems in Stoicism*, ed. A.A. Long (London, 1971) 17; A.A. Long, 'Language and thought in Stoicism', in *Problems in Stoicism*, 91, 110, n. 72; A. Graeser, *Zenon von Kition. Positionen und Probleme* (Berlin, 1975) 52; H. von Staden, 'The Stoic theory of perception and its "Platonic" critics', in *Studies in Perception*, ed. P.K. Machamer and R.G. Turnbull (Ohio, 1978) 99-136; G.B. Kerferd, 'The problem of *synkatathesis* and *katalepsis* in Stoic Doctrine', in *Les stoïciens et leur logique*, ed. J. Brunschwig (Paris, 1978) 270; J. Annas, 'Truth and Knowledge', in *Doubt and Dogmatism*, ed. M. Schofield, M. Burnyeat, J. Barnes (Oxford, 1980) 84-104.

[2] There may have been a discussion among the Stoics as to whether a *lekton* could be a *huparchon*. We are told that the Stoic Basilides denied the reality (*huparxis*) of the *lekton* on the grounds that the incorporeal was nothing (*SVF* 3, p. 268).

And when they are asked 'What is the *huparchon*?', they say that it is that which moves an apprehensive presentation. Then, when they are examined in regard to the apprehensive presentation, again they turn to the *huparchon*, although it is equally unknown, saying 'an apprehensive presentation is that which is from the *huparchon* in accordance with the *huparchon* itself' ... Since we know neither the former nor the latter, we shall not comprehend what is being explained from them, the true and false proposition (S.E. *Math.* 8.85-6).

A demonstrative argument was defined by Diogenes Laertius as 'an argument, which, by means of what is more clearly apprehended, concludes that which is less clearly apprehended' (D.L. 7.45 = 2.235). He says that an argument, according to the followers of Crinis, is that which is composed of a major premise (*lêmma*), a minor premise (*proslêpsis*) and a conclusion (*epiphora*), and gives us the following specification:

If it is day, then it is light (*lêmma*),
It is day (*proslêpsis*),
Therefore, it is light (*epiphora*, 7.76).

A passage in Sextus Empiricus provides conclusive proof that the minor premise is a *huparchon*:

Therefore, because he has a concept of logical consequence immediately, a man apprehends the *noêsis* (act of thinking) of sign because of the logical consequence; for the sign itself is of such a form: 'If this, then this.' That the sign is real (*huparchein*) follows from the nature and constitution of man (*Math.* 8.276 = 2.223).[3]

[3] For a discussion of this passage see Long (1971) 87, and M.F. Burnyeat, 'The origins of non-deductive inference', in *Science and Speculation*, ed. J. Barnes *et al.* (Cambridge, 1982) 206-17.

In spite of this statement by Sextus Empiricus, the sign may more properly be regarded as the antecedent of a conditional rather than the whole conditional. It seems better, therefore, to assume that the *noêsis* should be specified by 'If this, then this', and the sign by 'If this'. The sign is the *huparchon*.

Specifications for the minor premise that moved the apprehensive presentation may be found in Cicero's *De Natura Deorum*. For instance, we read: 'Further, the heavens and all the bodies which have an eternal order cannot be made by man; therefore, that by whom they are made is better than man; what would you call that except god?' (2.16 = *SVF* 2.1012). Here the minor premise is: 'They cannot be made by man.' This is the *huparchon* that moves the apprehensive presentation: 'That by whom they are made is better than man.'[4] Again, we find another argument that reads: 'For if indeed there are not any gods, what can there be in the universe better than man? For in him alone is reason, and nothing can be more outstanding than this. For a man to think that nothing in the whole world is better than man is foolish arrogance; therefore, there is something better; this, therefore, is certainly god' (2.16 = 2.1011). As Dragona-Monachou suggests, we may state the minor premise as: 'There is something in the whole world better than man.' The minor premise, a *huparchon*, moves the apprehensive presentation: 'This is certainly god.'[5]

How, then, can an incorporeal *lekton* (expressible) move a presentation? It could move a presentation, if it itself was presented as a presentation, for the Stoics regarded the presentation as a corporeal:

---

[4] M. Dragona-Monachou, *The Stoic Arguments for the Existence and the Providence of the Gods* (Athens, 1976) 114.
[5] ibid. 115.

For it is very absurd of them to make the virtues and the vices and all the skills and memories besides and presentations, moreover, and affections and impulses and assents corporeal, and to say that they do not reside or are real in anything (Plut. *Comm. Not.* 1084A).

Cherniss explained that, since they are all dispositions of the soul, and the soul is corporeal, they are all corporeal.[6] If, therefore, the proposition is presented to the ruling part of the soul as a corporeal, it would move an apprehensive presentation. We may surmise the following steps: (1) the proposition is formed by the *logos*, (2) the proposition appears to the ruling part of the soul as a rational presentation, (3) the ruling part of the soul apprehends the rational presentation through the *logos* (2.61, 84).

If, therefore, the proposition, as a presentation, moves the apprehensive presentation, the presentation itself must have propositional content. This topic was investigated in a recent article by Frede, who writes that 'the thought is the thought of a proposition; but it is characterized not only by the proposition it is a thought of, but also by the way this proposition is thought'.[7] He explains this by writing: 'For the same proposition may be thought in any number of ways, and depending on the way it is thought we get different kinds of impressions. One way they differ is the way in which the subject of the proposition – that is, the object of the thought – is represented in the impression. The thought that this (a book in front of me) is green which I have when I look at the book differs considerably from the thought that this (the very same book) is green which I have when I close

[6] *Plutarch's Moralia*, XIII, part 2, ed. H. Cherniss (Loeb, Harvard, 1976) 855, and 854, note d. For the corporeal see I. Mueller, 'Geometry and scepticism', in *Science and Speculation*, 74-7.

[7] M. Frede, 'Stoics and skeptics on clear and distinct impressions', in *The Skeptical Tradition*, ed. M. Burnyeat (California, 1983) 71.

my eyes and touch the book.'[8] If, therefore, thoughts form the content of impressions, and thoughts are thoughts of propositions, propositions form the content of impressions.

The evidence for the *huparchon* as an external entity is found in two passages, one in Sextus Empiricus, and the other in Diogenes Laertius:

The apprehensive presentation is (1) that which arises from a *huparchon*, and (2) which is stamped and impressed according to the *huparchon* itself, and (3) *which is such that it could not arise from that which is not a huparchon (apo mê huparchontos)*. (4) For assuming that this presentation is capable of apprehending that which underlies accurately, and receives as its impression all its particular features (*ta peri autois idiômata*) precisely, they say that each of these has an attribute (*sumbebêkos*), (*Math.* 7.248 = 2.65).

The apprehensive presentation, which, they say, is a criterion of things is that which arises from a *huparchon*, being stamped and impressed according to the *huparchon* itself (7.46 = 2.53, p. 21).

Hadot objected that, if the *huparchon* is an external object, one cannot understand why there should be a confusion in presentations which would cause us to give up the apprehensive presentation. He argued that we cannot identify the real corporeal object as the source of an apprehensive presentation with the characteristic of a true proposition. He defined the *huparchon* as follows: 'Huparchein bezeichnet daher letzlich das Charakteristikum eines aktuellen Prädikates, d.h. eines Prädikates,

---

8 Frede, 69. Coussin writes: 'et l'assentiment est donné à la proposition, non à la représentation, de sorte qu'une représentation persuasive est une représentation qui nous porte à donner l'assentiment à la proposition qu'elle implique.' P. Coussin, 'Le stoïcisme de la nouvelle académie', *Revue d'histoire de la philosophie* 3 (1929) 262. This article was reprinted in *The Skeptical Tradition*, 31-63.

das sich faktisch auf ein Subjekt bezieht, das ihm "zukommt".'[9] Hadot's objections cannot be brushed aside. If we assume that a material object is a *huparchon*, we have difficult questions to answer. If material objects move apprehensive presentations, and these presentations are necessarily true, how is misidentification possible at all, and why is it necessary for the wise man to suspend judgment when faced with a perceptive presentation? Further, if the material object moves an apprehensive presentation, why is assent to the apprehensive presentation necessary, and why do we have a statement in Sextus Empiricus to the effect that the perceptibles are true only with reference to the intelligibles that correspond to them (2.195)?

In spite of these reservations, we have to assume that an external entity, such as, Electra, was a *huparchon*. Sextus Empiricus' description of a true and false presentation reads as follows:

> True and false, as, for example, the one (sc. presentation) that fell upon Orestes in his madness which had its source in Electra (for inasmuch as it came from a *huparchon*, it was true, for Electra was real); but inasmuch as it came from a Fury, it was false, for she was not a Fury (Math. 7.244-5 = 2.65).

> For again, some (sc. presentations) are from a *huparchon*, but they do not resemble the *huparchon* itself (*ouk auto de to huparchon indallontai*), as we showed in the case of the mad Orestes a little earlier. For he formed a presentation from a *huparchon*, Electra (*apo huparchontos tês Êlektras*), not according to the *huparchon* itself (*Math*. 7.249 = 2.65).

Evidence that the proper name entailed the reality of the object of reference is found in the eighth Stoic amphiboly in Galen's *On Fallacies due to Language*:

[9] P. Hadot, 'Zur Vorgeschichte des Begriffs "Existenz" hyparchein bei den Stoikern', *Arch. f. Begriffsgeschichte* 13 (1969) 123.

The eighth is that which does not indicate what refers to what. For example, *DIÔNTHEÔNESTIN*, for it is not clear whether it refers to the *huparxis* (reality) of both or to some such thing as 'Dion is Theon', or the converse.[10]

The word *huparxis* (reality) seems to denote *Diôn huparchei* (Dion is real) or *Theon huparchei* (Theon is real). If this is correct, *Diôn esti* (Dion is) denotes *Diôn huparchei* (Dion is real), and Dion is a *huparchon*.

In the above specification, Sextus Empiricus was not concerned with the object of reference but with two attributes 'being real' and 'being a Fury'. Since 'being real' is a necessary attribute of Electra, he refers to Electra as 'being real'. If, therefore, the *huparchon* was not merely a corporeal body, but a corporeal body which had a particular attribute, we may now interpret the first two parts of Sextus Empiricus' definition of the apprehension which I quoted above: 'The apprehensive presentation is (1) that which arises from a *huparchon*, and (2) which is stamped and impressed according to the *huparchon* itself.' To say that a presentation is from a *huparchon* is to say that it has its source in a corporeal body. If, however, it is 'according to the *huparchon* itself', it corresponds to the attribute which is present in the body.

Several passages support this interpretation. First, Diogenes Laertius specifies the apprehension, and consequently the apprehensive presentation, by 'The gods have providence', or 'The gods exist' (2.84). That which moved the apprehensive presentation, therefore, was not simply 'the gods', but 'the gods having providence', or 'the gods existing'. Further, in their definition of the definite proposition, the Stoics declared that the definite proposition 'This man is sitting', or 'This man is walking' is true, when the predicate 'sitting' or 'walking' is the attribute of the object of reference (2.205,

[10] R.B. Edlow, *Galen on Language and Ambiguity* (Leiden, 1977) 108.

cf. 509). The attribute and the predicate were closely connected. They shared a particular corporeal body as a common source (1.89). If, therefore, the predicate in the proposition moved the apprehensive presentation, it would seem to follow that the attribute moved it also.

Kerferd, however, suggested that the *huparchon* is 'a material object qua *idiôs poion* (individual qualification)'.[11] The suggestion is interesting, and it does account for the qualitative aspects of the *huparchon*. Many of the individual qualifications, however, are not perceptible. I cannot perceive, for instance, that a man is a runner or that he had been posted in an advanced position at some earlier time. Qualifications of this type do not seem sufficient to move an apprehensive presentation.

Particularly relevant to our discussion is a sentence in Sextus Empiricus: 'For assuming that this presentation is capable of apprehending that which underlies accurately, and receives as its impression all its particular features (*ta peri autois idiômata*) precisely, they say that each of these has an attribute (*sumbebêkos*, *Math*. 7.248 = 2.65). If the term *idiômata* was related to *idion*, the *idion* (essential characteristic) was corporeal and connected in some way with the attribute. Chrysippus defined a definition as 'the assigning of the essential characteristic' (2.226). I have interpreted this as the assigning of the essential characteristic (*idion*) to the qualification (*poion*), and I have argued that the term to be defined was either the individual quality or the individual qualification. It seems unlikely, however, that the two terms were connected. Rather, the *idiômata* were probably synonymous with the *sumbebêkota* (attributes).

In my translation of Sextus Empiricus, *Math*. 7.248 (above, p. 75), I italicized a clause which read: 'which is such that it could not arise from that which is not a *huparchon* (*apo mê huparchontos*)'. Rist translated the

---

[11] Kerferd (1978) 270.

phrase as 'of such a kind as could not come from what is
not that existing object'.[12] His translation was challenged
by Graeser on the grounds that it was not supported by
Sextus Empiricus, *Math.* 7.248-51, or Cicero, *Acad. Pr.*
11, 77.[13] Von Staden translated it as: 'Of such a kind that
it could not occur from an object that does not exist.'[14] He
equated it with *ab eo quod non est* (from that which is
not) in *Acad. Pr.* 11, 77: 'Here, Zeno perceived acutely
that there was no presentation that could be perceived, if
that which arises from that which is (*ab eo quod est*)
could be of such a kind that that which arises from that
which is not (*ab eo quod non est*) could be of the same
kind.'[15]

Where can we find a presentation which is such that it
could arise from 'that which is not real'? We may, I
believe, find such a presentation in the false presentation, which Sextus Empiricus defines as follows: 'False
(sc. presentations) are those of which it is possible to
make a false statement, as, for example, that the oar in
the water is broken or that the stoa is foreshortened'
(*Math.* 7.244 = 2.65).

Diogenes Laertius defined the apprehensive presentation and the non-apprehensive as follows:

The apprehensive presentation which, they say, is a
criterion of things is (1) that which arises from a
huparchon, and (2) is stamped and impressed according
to the *huparchon* itself; non-apprehensive (*akatalêpton*)
is (1) that which does not arise from a *huparchon* (*tên mê
apo huparchontos*) or (2) that which arises from a
huparchon but is not according to the *huparchon* itself. (3)
It is not clearly impressed (7.46 = 2.53, p.21).

[12] Rist (1969) 137.
[13] A. Graeser, review of J.M. Rist, *Stoic Philosophy*, in *Gnomon* 44 (1972) 17.
[14] Von Staden (1978) 102.
[15] ibid. 103-5.

Von Staden connected the words 'that which does not arise from a *huparchon*' in Diogenes' first definition of the non-apprehensive with *ex eo unde non esset* in Cicero's *Acad. Pr.* 11, 18: 'a presentation stamped and impressed from that from which it was (*ex eo, unde esset*) such that it could not be from that from which it was not (*ex eo, unde non esset*).'[16] Specifying this kind of presentation, von Staden wrote: 'a presentation x at t_1 from (*apo*) the existing (i.e. also present) object Emma might be mistaken for a presentation y of her (absent) "identical" twin Ella.'[17]

The two expressions: Sextus Empiricus' 'from that which is not a *huparchon* (*apo mê huparchontos*)' and Diogenes Laertius' 'that which is not from a *huparchon* (*tên mê apo huparchontos*)', seem to denote false presentations. We may specify Sextus' phrase by the false presentation 'the oar in the water is broken'. Diogenes' is less certain. It seems difficult to assume that Diogenes' phrase indicated misrepresentations only. It may, in fact, have covered much more than false presentations, and included all presentations which were not apprehensive. Diogenes' second definition probably refers to a true and false presentation, such as 'Electra is a Fury'. We should notice that Diogenes' definitions of the non-apprehensive might very well apply to value judgments. The presentation 'Pleasure is a good' is a possible specification for a false presentation, described as 'which is not from a *huparchon*', and a presentation such as 'The good is inexpedient' may be a specification for a presentation which is true and false.

Commenting on the clause 'which is such that it could not arise from that which is not a *huparchon*', Sextus Empiricus wrote: 'They added "such that it could not arise from that which is not a *huparchon*", because the members of the Academy did not assume, as the Stoics

16 ibid. 104.
17 ibid. 101.

did, that it was impossible that any (sc. presentation) precisely similar (*apparallakton tina*) in all respects should be found (*Math.* 7.252 = 2.65). This sentence is explained by a passage in Plutarch's *De Communibus Notitiis* (1077C) in which Plutarch states that one can find many passages where the Stoics 'are crying out that the latter (i.e. the Academics) confuse all things with their indistinguishable likenesses (*tais aparallaxiais*), by urging that there is one qualified entity in two substances'. Plutarch goes on to say that there is not any man who does not believe and think, on the contrary, that it is amazing and paradoxical if in all time there have not been two doves, or two grains of wheat or two figs, as the proverb goes, precisely similar to each other.[18]

According to Sextus Empiricus, Zeno was arguing that an apprehensive presentation was such that it could not arise from x (e.g. the stone being smooth), if, in fact, it arose from y (the stone being rough). What is more, it is such that it could not arise from x (e.g. being smooth) in object m, if it came from y (being smooth) in object n. Words such as 'being smooth', therefore, have the connotation 'being smooth in m'. Accordingly, the proposition 'The stone is smooth' should be interpreted as meaning 'This "being smooth" belongs to m'.

The word 'indistinguishable' was applied to individuals in the Stoic theory of recurrence. The Stoics held that, although presentations were not indistinguishable one from another, a presentation in one cyclic nexus was indistinguishable from a corresponding presentation in another cyclic nexus. Origen says, however, that those of the Stoics who were embarrassed by this doctrine admitted 'a small and very brief deviation' (2.626). If, of course, there was a slight deviation, that in which the deviation occurred was not indistinguishable.

How, then, are we to explain the very exceptional

---

[18] Cherniss (1976) 799, note f.

power of the apprehensive presentation to apprehend that which underlies? The explanation probably lies in medicine. Frede drew attention to a doctrine in Hellenistic medicine which may be Stoic in origin in which 'the discriminatory power of the senses far outruns the ability of the mind to conceptualize the object'.[19]

---

[19] Frede (1983) 76-7.

7

The *Logos* that Selects

In the third book of Cicero's *De Finibus* we find a passage which recognizes the act of 'retaining those things that are according to nature and rejecting those that are the contrary' as an appropriate act, and distinguishes several kinds of selection. What were the different kinds of appropriate acts recognized by the Stoics, and how should we explain the various kinds of selection to which Cicero refers? These are the questions that I shall try to answer in the first part of this chapter. In the second half, I shall consider the three kinds of rational impulse, desire, reasonable desire, and choice, the objects towards which they were directed, and the hormetic presentations that moved them. Finally, I shall discuss the relationship between the predicates and the terms for joy and pleasure that correspond to them.

> Therefore, with our first principles thus established, that those things which are according to nature ought to be taken up for their own sake, and their contraries likewise rejected, the first appropriate act (for so I translated *kathêkon*) is to preserve oneself in one's natural state, secondly, to hold those things that are according to nature and reject the contrary; when this selection and likewise rejection has been found (1), there follows next (2) selection in conjunction with an appropriate act, then (3) that (sc. selection) which is lasting, and (4) that which is

completely constant and in harmony with nature (*Fin.* 3.6.21-2).[1]

Cicero defines the first appropriate act as preserving oneself in one's natural state, and the second as holding those things that are according to nature and rejecting the contrary. He then goes on to list four kinds of selection. The first kind of selection is synonymous with 'holding those things that are according to nature and rejecting the contrary'. The first appropriate act, therefore, is not an act of selecting but a movement towards that which belongs to it:

> They say that the first impulse which an animal has is directed towards preserving oneself, since from the very beginning its nature 'belongs' to it. Just as Chrysippus says in the first book of his *Concerning Ends*, when he asserts that his own constitution and his awareness of this are the first thing which 'belongs' to every animal (3.178).[2]

[1] Pembroke wrote that the third book of the *De Finibus* was generally believed to derive from an orthodox handbook in the time of Diogenes of Babylon or Antipater of Tarsus. G.S. Pembroke, '*Oikeiôsis*', in *Problems in Stoicism*, ed. A.A. Long (London, 1971) 120, 143, n. 31. Kerferd, however, argued that there was reason to suppose that the material in *De Finibus* 3.5.16f. flowed from the same ultimate source as the passage in Diogenes Laertius 7.85 (*SVF* 3.178), and that this was likely to be the work of Chrysippus cited by Diogenes Laertius: see G.B. Kerferd, 'The search for personal identity in Stoic thought', *Bulletin of the John Rylands University Library of Manchester* 55 (1972) 185.

[2] For a discussion of *oikeiôsis* (the process by which an animal comes to terms with itself and its environment) see M. Pohlenz, 'Grundfragen der Stoischen Philosophie', *Abh. Ges. Wiss. Göttingen Phil.-hist. Kl.* 3, 26 (1940) 1-81; Pembroke (1971) 114-49; A.A. Long, 'The logical basis of Stoic ethics', *Proc. Arist. Soc.* 71 (1970-1) 97-101; Kerferd (1972) 177-96; A. Graeser, *Zenon von Kition. Positionen und Probleme* (Berlin, 1975) 176-87; H. Görgemanns, '*Oikeiôsis* in Arius Didymus', in *On Stoic and Peripatetic Ethics. The Work of Arius Didymus*, ed. W.W. Fortenbaugh, *Rutgers University Studies in Classical Humanities* 1 (1982) 183-7; B. Inwood, 'Comments on Professor Görgemanns' paper', 193-201; B. Inwood, 'Hierocles: theory and argument in the second century AD', *Oxford Studies in Ancient Philosophy* 2 (1984) 151-83; J. Brunschwig, 'The cradle argument', in *The Norms of Nature*, ed. M.

There is a difficult transition between the act of preserving oneself in one's natural state, and holding those things that are according to nature and rejecting their contrary in both Cicero and the passage from Diogenes Laertius which I quoted above. This passage continues with the words:

> In addition, when in the case of animals the impulse supervenes,[3] and they are enabled by this to move towards that which belongs (*ta oikeia*), that which is according to nature falls to their lot, in so far as they are being directed according to the impulse (3.178).

Alexander of Aphrodisias seems to have recognized a close relation between 'those things according to nature' and 'that which belongs', for he writes: 'The function of virtue concerned with the selection of those things according to nature and belonging' (3.766), and 'Nature because of the selection of these things (sc. these things that are according to nature), since they belong to us, apprehends virtue' (3.194).

In the *Ethike Stoicheiosis*, a treatise by the philosopher Hierocles, a Stoic of the second century AD, we find evidence for a connection between *oikeiôsis* (the process by which an animal comes to terms with itself and its environment) and 'those things that are according to nature', and a progression from 'those things that are according to nature' to the goods.[4] Hierocles refers to an *oikeiôsis* which is capable of exercising choice with respect to external objects and says that we 'belong' to external objects through choice. Kerferd has drawn

---

Schofield, G. Striker (Cambridge, 1986) 128-44; G. Striker, 'The role of *oikeiôsis* in Stoic ethics', *Oxford Studies in Ancient Philosophy* 1 (1938) 145-67.

[3] For *epigignomenês* see O. Brink, '*Oikeiôsis* and *oikeiotês*. Theophrastus and Zeno on nature in moral theory', *Phronesis* 1 (1956) 132-45.

[4] Hierokles, *Ethische Elementarlehre*, ed. H. von Arnim, *Berliner Klassiker-texte* 4 (Berlin, 1906).

attention to the words *oikeiôsis hairetikê* (*oikeiôsis* capable of choosing) in Hierocles (col. 9, 5-8), and argued that Hierocles probably equated it with *hairesis eklektikê* (choice capable of selecting, col. 9,10).[5] There are, however, significant differences in the terminology used by Hierocles and that used by the philosophers of the early Stoa. The object of *hairesis* (choice, or the act of choosing) in the early Stoa was the *haireteon* (that which ought to be chosen), as, for example, *to phronein* (thinking wisely). The possession of 'those things according to nature' was not classified as 'that which ought to be chosen'.

The Stoics described a 'preferred' as 'that which we select, although it is an indifferent, according to a directing *logos*' (3.128). Diogenes Laertius specifies 'the preferreds' in one passage by life, health, pleasure, beauty, strength, wealth, a good reputation and good birth (3.117), and in another by wealth, a good reputation, health and strength (3.119). The *logos* selects *x*, for example, pleasure, from the indifferents, a term which denotes the class of objects which includes 'the preferreds' and their contraries, 'the rejecteds'. The *logos* formed a proposition, such as 'Pleasure is an indifferent', or the propositional content of the presentation. That pleasure is an indifferent is well attested in our sources (3.117). 'The preferreds' were identified with 'things according to nature', and 'the rejecteds' with 'things contrary to nature'. 'The preferreds', or 'those things according to nature' are capable of moving an impulse (3.119, 3.121).

We read in Stobaeus that 'those things that are according to nature' are 'acceptable' (*lêpta*), and all 'those things that are contrary to nature' are not. Of 'those things that are according to nature' some are acceptable in them-

---

[5] Col. 9,3-8 was quoted by Pembroke, 144, n. 59, and discussed by Kerferd (1972) 191-2. The term *sungenikê oikeiôsis* appears in *Ethike Stoicheiosis* (col. 9,3-4); *kêdemonikê oikeiôsis* in the *Anonymous Commentary on the Theaetetus* (cols. 7,28 and 8,5-6). For these terms see Kerferd (1972) 194.

selves, others through other things. In themselves are whatever are capable of moving an impulse towards themselves, for example, health, keenness of perception, freedom from pain and beauty of body; productive are those that are capable of moving an impulse towards other things, for example, wealth, reputation and things similar to these (3.142). Since 'things according to nature' are 'acceptable', we have to assume that a presentation, such as, ' "This" (e.g. health) is acceptable', was followed by an 'accepting' (*lêpsis*) directed towards 'that which ought to be accepted' (*lêpteon*). Whether the *lêpsis* was an impulse is a matter of doubt. It is never called so in any of our sources.

A story told about the Stoic philosopher Sphaerus is particularly important for any reconstruction of the steps leading to the movement of the impulse. When Sphaerus reached out his hand for the pomegranates, the king exclaimed that he had given assent to a false presentation, but Sphaerus replied that he had given assent not to their being pomegranates but to its being reasonable that they were pomegranates (*houtôs sunkatatetheisthai, ouch' hoti rhoai eisin, all' hoti eulogon esti rhoas autas einai*, 1.625, cf. 624). We may reconstruct the presentation that moves the impulse by ' "This" is a pomegranate', or ' "This" is acceptable (*lêpton*)'. This was followed by the rational impulse's giving assent to the proposition: 'It is reasonable that "this" is a pomegranate', and its movement towards that which ought to be accepted (*lêpteon*). All impulses were assents (3.171). In this instance, the movement of the rational impulse may be accompanied by the movement of the practical impulse, the stretching out of the hand towards the pomegranate.

Stobaeus distinguishes between the *lêpton* (acceptable) and the *haireton* (choiceworthy), but because of a lacuna in the text it is impossible to determine with any certainty how he explained the difference between the two terms:

They say that the choiceworthy and the acceptable are different. For the choiceworthy is that which is capable of moving a complete impulse (*hormês autotelous*), <but the acceptable (*lêpton*) is that which we select reasonably>. But to such a degree as the choiceworthy differs from the acceptable, the choiceworthy <by> itself differs from the acceptable by itself, and, generally, the good from that which has value (3.131).

Wachsmuth filled the lacuna with the words: *lêpton de ho eulogistôs eklegometha*; his emendation was accepted by von Arnim. Long pointed out that the emendation was based on the definition of the *telos* offered by Diogenes of Babylon, and expressed some misgivings about its validity.[6] He also emended *autotelous* (complete) to *autotelôs* (completely) in the third line of the text.[7]

The presentations: ' "This" is acceptable (*lêpton*)', or ' "This" is choiceworthy', resemble the conclusion of the rational argument, for example:

If there are pleasures, they are indifferents,
'This' is a pleasure,
'This' is an indifferent.

or

If there are absolutely appropriate acts (*katorthô-mata*), they are choiceworthy,
'This' is an absolutely appropriate act,
'This' is choiceworthy.[8]

---

[6] A.A. Long, 'The early Stoic concept of moral choice', in *Images of Man in Ancient and Medieval Thought. Studia Gerardo Verbeke*, ed. F. Bossier, F. De Wachter *et al*. (Leuven, 1976) 82, n. 6.

[7] ibid. 83.

[8] For this type of argument and its relation to the presentation see C. Imbert, 'Stoic logic and Alexandrian poetics', in *Doubt and Dogmatism. Studies in Hellenistic Epistemology*, ed. M. Schofield, M. Burnyeat, J. Barnes (Oxford, 1982) 192.

The minor premise of the argument, a *huparchon* (that-which-is-real), moves the apprehensive presentation, ' "This" is an indifferent', or ' "This" is choiceworthy' (S.E. *Math*. 8.85-6; 8.276 = *SVF* 2.223).[9]

At the beginning of this chapter, I drew attention to the four kinds of selection which were indicated in Cicero's *De Finibus* (3.6.21-2): (1) selection; (2) selection in conjunction with an appropriate act; (3) selection which is lasting, in conjunction with an appropriate act; (4) selection which is completely constant and in harmony with nature, in conjunction with an appropriate act. What are the appropriate acts to which Cicero is referring, and how should we explain the last three kinds of selection?

Appropriate acts (*kathêkonta*) are defined as 'what the *logos* chooses to do, for example, to honour one's parents, brothers and fatherland, and to assist one's friends' (3.495), or as 'that which is in conformity with (sc. *logos*) in one's way of life, for whose action a reasonable account (*eulogon apologian*) can be given' (3.494). The *katorthôma* is an absolutely appropriate act (3.500).[10] I have drawn attention to a diaeresis of *kathêkonta* (appropriate acts) and *katorthômata* (absolutely appropriate acts) in Stobaeus (*Ec*. II, p. 85,18-86,16):[11]

---

[9] For further discussion see pp. 72-3.

[10] For a discussion of appropriate acts and absolutely appropriate acts see I.G. Kidd, 'Stoic intermediates and the end for man', in *Problems in Stoicism*, 150-72; I.G. Kidd, 'Moral actions and rules in Stoic ethics', in *The Stoics*, ed. J.M. Rist (California, 1978) 247-58; G.B. Kerferd, 'Cicero and Stoic ethics', in *Cicero and Vergil. Studies in Honour of Harold Hunt*, ed. J.R.C. Martyn (Amsterdam, 1972) 60-74; T. Engberg-Pedersen, 'Discovering the good: *oikeiôsis* and *kathêkonta* in Stoic ethics', in *The Norms of Nature*, ed. M. Schofield, G. Striker (Cambridge, 1978) 172.

[11] M.E. Reesor, 'On the Stoic goods in Stobaeus, *Eclogae* 2', in *On Stoic and Peripatetic Ethics. The Work of Arius Didymus*, 77-8.

kathêkonta
(appropriate acts)

teleia kathêkonta or
katorthômata
(absolutely
appropriate acts)

mesa kathêkonta
(intermediate
appropriate acts, e.g.
to marry, to serve as an
ambassador)

hôn chrê
(belonging to those
that necessarily
are)

ta d'ou i.e. *ouch hôn chrê*
(not belonging to those that
necessarily are)

Stobaeus' source specifies *hôn chrê* by *to phronein* (thinking wisely) and *to sôphronein* (acting moderately, 3.503). He also writes that 'that which ought to be chosen' can be specified by *to phronein* (thinking wisely, 3.89). 'That which ought to be chosen', therefore, is the 'absolutely appropriate act' (the *katorthôma*). The term *ouch hôn chrê* (not belonging to those that necessarily are) may be specified by 'honouring one's parents' and 'honouring one's fatherland', on the basis of a passage in Diogenes Laertius which reads: 'Appropriate acts, then, are what the *logos* chooses to do, such as, for example, to honour one's parents, brothers, fatherland, and to assist one's friends' (3.495). I would suggest that these are the *boulêtea* (those things which ought to be reasonably desired). If this is the case, we may suppose that the *orektea* (those things which ought to be desired) correspond to the intermediate appropriate acts.

We are now able to specify the four kinds of selection mentioned by Cicero (*Fin.* 3.6.21-2):

(1) selection: ' "This" (e.g. pleasure) is an indifferent.'
(2) selection in conjunction with the appropriate act: ' "This" (e.g to marry, to serve as an ambassador) is an intermediate appropriate act.'
(3) selection which is lasting, in conjunction with the appropriate act: ' "This" (e.g. to honour one's parents, to

honour one's fatherland) is an appropriate act.'

(4) selection which is completely constant and in harmony with nature, in conjunction with the appropriate act: ' "This" (e.g. thinking wisely, acting moderately) is an absolutely appropriate act.'

In Stobaeus we read that 'that which moves the impulse is nothing other than an immediate hormetic presentation of what is appropriate (*kathêkon*)' (3.169). Since the appropriate act is that which ought to be desired (*orekteon*), that which ought to be reasonably desired (*boulêteon*), and that which ought to be chosen (*haireteon*), the presentation that moves the impulse ought to be specified with these terms, for example, ' "This" (absolutely appropriate act) ought to be chosen.'

The *orexis* (desire) is a species of the rational impulse (3.169). *Boulêsis* was defined as *eulogos orexis* (reasonable desire, 3.432), and *epithumia* as *alogos orexis* (unaccountable desire, 3.391). Graeser has drawn attention to two passages in Galen which cast light on the meaning of *alogos*:[12]

Therefore, not incorrectly is the emotion of the soul said by some to be a movement contrary to nature, as is the case in regard to fear, appetite and other such things. All such movements and states are disobedient to the *logos* and turned aside with respect to it (De Lacy IV. 4.16-17).

We must interpret this, *to alogon*, as 'disobedient to the *logos* and turned aside with respect to the *logos*', for according to this movement and by habit we say that someone is pressing forward and moving unaccountably (*alogôs*) apart from the judgment of the *logou* (*aneu logou kriseôs*, IV.2.12).

[12] Graeser (1975) 147. For *alogon* see also M. Dragona-Monachou, *The Stoic Arguments for the Existence and Providence of the Gods* (Athens, 1976) 48-9.

All three 'good emotions' (*eupatheiai*) contain the word 'reasonable' (*eulogos*) in their definitions: *boulêsis* is reasonable desire (*eulogos orexis*), precaution (*eulabeia*) is reasonable disinclination (*eulogos ekklisis*), and joy (*chara*) is reasonable elation (*eulogos eparsis*, 3.432). We may assume that all three were movements 'obedient to the *logos*', and 'not turned aside with respect to the *logos*'.[13]

The term *hairesis* (choice) was defined by Stobaeus as *boulêsis ex analogismou* (reasonable desire based on analogy, 3.173). Galen defines *analogismos* as 'a *logos* which has its starting point in the phenomena and makes an apprehension (*katalêpsis*) of that which is unclear' (2.269). Since the *hairesis* (choice) is a *boulêsis* (reasonable desire), we may expect to find the phenomena which are under consideration in the *boulêtea* (those things which ought to be reasonably desired), such as, for example, 'honouring one's parents', or 'honouring one's fatherland'. In other words, the phenomena are the appropriate acts. My interpretation of analogy is supported by a passage in which Sextus Empiricus shows how the concepts of Cyclops and Pygmy are formed. They were formed by analogy, by increasing and decreasing the size of ordinary men (*Math.* 4.42).[14] The terms are abstractions from sense data. An apprehensive presentation, such as ' "This act" ought to be chosen', is the apprehensive presentation to which Galen is refering.

Stobaeus outlines the role of the 'choiceworthy' (*haireton*) in a passage which reads:

[13] The term *eulogos*, which played such an important role in the Stoic process of decision, is found in some very interesting passages which have been collected by De Lacy: P.H. De Lacy, 'Comments on Professor Kidd's paper', in *On Stoic and Peripatetic Ethics. The Work of Arius Didymus*, 115-16. See also G. Striker, 'Sceptical strategies', in *Doubt and Dogmatism*, ed. M. Schofield, M. Burnyeat, J. Barnes (Oxford, 1980) 65-6.

[14] For this passage see I. Mueller, 'Geometry and scepticism', in *Science and Speculation*, ed. J. Barnes *et al.* (Cambridge, 1982) 78. See also E. Grumach, *Physis und Agathon in der alten Stoa. Problemata* 6 (1932) 6-8; and A.-J. Voelke, *L'idée de volonté dans le stoïcisme* (Paris, 1973) 65.

The 'choiceworthy' is everything good and 'that which ought to be chosen' is every benefit (*ôphelêma*) which is recognized as equivalent to the possession of the good.[15] Because of this we choose 'that which ought to be chosen', for example, 'thinking wisely' (*to phronein*), which is recognized as equivalent to the possession of practical wisdom (*phronêsis*, 3.89).

In a passage that I quoted earlier Stobaeus wrote that 'the choiceworthy is that which is capable of moving a complete impulse' (3.131). It seems then that we have two presentations that move the impulse: ' "This" (e.g. virtue) is choiceworthy', and ' "This" (e.g. thinking wisely) ought to be chosen'. These would be followed by an act of assent, given by the impulse, to the proposition: 'It is reasonable that "this" ought to be chosen', and by a movement of the impulse (the act of choosing, *hairesis*) towards that which ought to be chosen (*haireteon*), the possession of virtue or activity according to virtue. Presentations representing the general principle as well as the specific instance seem to have been required. The Stoics distinguished between *orekton* and *orekteon* (the desirable and that which ought to be desired), *boulêton* and *boulêteon* (the reasonably desirable and that which ought to be reasonably desired), the *apodekton* and *apodekteon* (the receivable and that which ought to be received) as well as the *haireton* and the *haireteon*. These pairs of terms should all be interpreted in the same way.

Chrysippus wrote that endurance and self-control were dispositions capable of following the *logos* that exercises

---

[15] The words *ho theôreitai para to echein to agathon*, which I have translated as 'which is recognized as equivalent to the possession of the good' were translated by Long as 'which is understood to depend upon the possession of the good'. See A.A. Long, 'The early Stoic concept of moral choice', in *Images of Man in Ancient and Medieval Thought. Studia Gerardo Verbeke*, ed. F. Bossier *et al.* (Leuven, 1976) 87; and M.E. Reesor, 'On the Stoic goods in Stobaeus, *Eclogae* 2', in *On Stoic and Peripatetic Ethics. The Work of Arius Didymus*, 78.

choice (3.384).[16] Since the cardinal virtues, wisdom, justice, courage and temperance, are described as dispositions (*hexeis*, Stob. *Ec.* II, p. 73, 1-15), or fixed dispositions (*diatheseis*, *SVF* 3.104), the cardinal virtues also are dispositions that are capable of following the *logos* that exercises choice. It is not at all clear whether the *logos* that exercises choice is the *logos* that forms presentations, such as ' "This" (i.e. virtue) is choiceworthy', and ' "This" (e.g. thinking wisely) ought to be chosen', or the impulse that moves towards that which ought to be chosen. The former seems more likely.

In a diaeresis in Stobaeus the goods are divided into virtues, and those that are not virtues, and the virtues, in turn, into those that are exact knowledge and crafts, and those that are not (*Ec.* II, p. 58,5-14). Diogenes Laertius defines exact knowledge as 'a disposition in the receiving of presentations, made unchangeable by *logos*' (1.68, 2.130). Stobaeus gives a similar definition (*Ec.* II, p. 74,1-2). Galen phrases the definition differently: 'Exact knowledge is a disposition, made unchangeable by *logos*, providing a belief on the basis of presentations, in a manner not blameworthy' (2.93). The *logos* which is mentioned in these passages is the *logos* that exercises choice. The virtue follows upon, and is held fast by this *logos*.

Exact knowledge is also defined as an apprehension (*katalêpsis*) reliable and made unchangeable by *logos*, or a composite from such apprehensions (Stob. *Ec.* II, p. 73,19-74,3). Exact knowledge, therefore, is a composite of apprehensions, and a disposition of the soul, whose stability is guaranteed by the *logos*. The apprehension gives assent to the apprehensive presentations. Each of the four cardinal virtues is exact knowledge. Each gives assent to an apprehensive presentation, such as ' "This" (i.e. virtue) is choiceworthy', and ' "This act" (e.g.

---

[16] I have inferred the translation 'the *logos* that exercises choice' from D.L. 7.108 = *SVF* 3.495.

thinking wisely) ought to be chosen'. The latter is the hormetic presentation that moves the impulse towards that which ought to be chosen.

My interpretation helps to explain why the appropriate act and virtue appear together in a passage in Plutarch:

> 'From where, then,' he says, 'shall I begin? And what shall I take as a starting point of the appropriate act and matter of virtue, if I pass over nature and that which is according to nature?' (3.491, cf. 3.64).

Bonhöffer and Dyroff assigned these sentences to Chrysippus.[17] The impulse, as choice, or the act of choosing, moves towards that which ought to be chosen, the absolutely appropriate act. The virtue, as an apprehension, or a composite of apprehensions, gives assent to the hormetic presentation, ' "This act" ought to be chosen', which moves the impulse. It follows upon the *logos* that forms the presentation.

The movement of the practical impulse cannot be separated from the movement of the rational impulse. The practical impulse is assent and movement:

> Assents are to some propositions, but impulses are to predicates which are evidenced in some way in the propositions to which the assents are given (3.171).

The meaning of this sentence can be inferred from a passage in Seneca:

> Every rational animal does nothing unless he has first been aroused by the appearance of something; then, he receives an impulse, and then assent confirms this impulse. I shall tell you what assent is. 'It is fitting for me

---

[17] A. Bonhöffer, *Die Ethik des Stoikers Epictet* (Stuttgart, 1894) 185; and A. Dyroff, *Die Ethik der alten Stoa* (Berlin, 1897, repr. 1979) 139, n. 3.

to walk.'[18] Then, at last I walk, when I have stated this to myself and approved this belief of mine (3.169).

For the practical impulse we must suppose a perceptive presentation, such as 'The enemy is attacking'. This would be followed by an act of assent, given by the impulse, to the proposition: 'It is fitting to resist the attack of the enemy', and by the movement of the practical impulse, 'Resisting the attack of the enemy'. The various steps leading up to the movement of the practical impulse, however, proceed concurrently with the steps leading to the movement of the rational impulse towards that which ought to be rationally desired. We may, therefore, construct two diagrams illustrating these steps:

A
The rational impulse

'This' (i.e. one's life) is an   'This act' (i.e. the appropriate act)
indifferent.   ought to be reasonably desired.

These presentations are followed by an act of assent on the part of the rational impulse to the proposition: 'It is reasonable that "this" (i.e. the appropriate act) ought to be reasonably desired', and by the movement of the impulse (reasonable desire, *boulêsis*) towards that which ought to be reasonably desired (*boulêteon*).

B
The practical impulse

The enemy is attacking

This presentation is followed by an act of assent on the part of the practical impulse to the proposition: 'It is fitting to resist the attack of the enemy', and by the

---

[18] For 'it is fitting *kathêkei*' see Long (above, n. 15) 91.

movement of the practical impulse, 'resisting the attack of the enemy'. The act of resisting the attack of the enemy cannot proceed independently of the movement of the rational impulse towards that which ought to be reasonably desired.

To conclude this chapter I shall consider the relation between the predicates, that which ought to be desired, that which ought to be reasonably desired, and that which ought to be chosen, and the various terms for pleasure and joy. De Lacy has successfully restored Chrysippus' definition of desire. According to his emendation, Galen wrote: 'Thus he defines desire (*orexis*) as a rational impulse towards something that gives pleasure to the extent that it should (*horizetai goun autên hormên logikên epi ti<nos> hoson chrê hêdon<tos>*).[19] How could 'that which ought to be desired (*orekteon*)' be both an appropriate act and 'that which gives pleasure to the extent that it should'?

We have two presentations that move the impulse: ' "This" (pleasure) is an indifferent', and ' "This" (i.e. the intermediate appropriate act) ought to be desired'. The desire (*orexis*, a rational impulse) gives assent to the proposition: 'It is reasonable that "this" (intermediate appropriate act) should be desired.' The assent is followed by the movement of the impulse towards that which ought to be desired, that is, that which gives pleasure to the extent that it should. The words *hoson chrê* (to the extent that it should) signify the restrictions placed upon *to hêdon* (that which gives pleasure) by the presentation ' "This" (i.e. pleasure) is an indifferent', and the nature of the appropriate act itself. The *orekteon* (that which ought to be desired) entails *to hêdon hoson chrê* (that which gives pleasure to the extent that it should).

We are told that pleasure supervenes after nature has sought what is suitable for its own constitution:

---

[19] De Lacy, IV. 2.4, IV. 4.2, V. 7.29.

> For, they say, pleasure is something which supervenes
> (*epigennêma*), if indeed there is such a thing, which
> nature receives, after it has sought what is suitable for its
> constitution ... In addition, when in the case of living
> creatures the impulse supervenes, and they are enabled
> by this to move towards that which belongs, *that which is*
> *according to nature* falls to their lot, in so far as they are
> being directed by the impulse (3.178).

It has not been generally realized how difficult the
interpretation of this passage really is. We seem to have
three possible interpretations of 'pleasure'. First, we may
assume that pleasure, an elation, followed the presentation ' "This" (e.g. what is suitable for my own
constitution) belongs', and preceded the movement of the
impulse towards that which belongs. In that case, the
words 'having sought' refer to the apprehension of the
presentation. 'That which is according to nature' in the
second half of the quotation may simply denote such
things as health or strength. Secondly, we may suppose
that pleasure, an elation, followed upon the movement of
the impulse towards that which belongs. This, I believe,
is incorrect, for the evidence places the elation after the
presentation and prior to the impulse.[20] The third
possibility is that pleasure was not regarded as an
elation at all in this passage, and that this pleasure was
something which supervened upon the movement of the
impulse towards that which belonged. If we use this
interpretation, we have to suppose two kinds of pleasure,
the pleasure that was an elation, and the pleasure that
was a supervention. This in itself seems very unlikely. I
would, therefore, decide in favour of the first hypothesis.
Gosling and Taylor assumed that pleasure accompanied
the possession of that which belongs: 'Pleasure is merely
something additional which occurs when each nature

[20] See pp. 130-1.

achieves that state which best fits its own constitution.'[21]
Since the apprehension of the presentation, the elation,
and the movement of the impulse towards that which
belongs must be an ongoing process, it seems better to
say that pleasure accompanied the act of seeking that
which belongs.

If we had any doubt that the Stoics recognized a
natural pleasure it would be dispelled by a passage in
Alexander's *Commentary on Aristotle's Topics*:

> Prodicus tried to assign to each of these words some
> essential characteristic indicated, just as the Stoics did,
> saying that joy is reasonable elation, pleasure unaccoun-
> table elation, that gladness is the pleasure which has its
> source in hearing, and enjoyment the pleasure which has
> its source in words (3.434).

Fragstein emended the last three words of the Greek to
read: 'which has its source in vision'.[22]

In Ps.-Andronicus' *Concerning Emotions*, joy (*chara*) is
defined as a reasonable elation (*eulogos eparsis*).[23] Since
the elation seems to have occurred between the
presentation and the impulse, the reasonable elation
must have followed an apprehensive presentation, such
as ' "This act" ought to be chosen', and arisen prior to the
impulse. The word *eulogos* (reasonable) suggests that the
elation was in accord with a proposition, such as 'It is
reasonable that "this act" ought to be chosen'.

'Joy' and 'gladness' were recognized as 'goods', but they
were carefully distinguished from the virtues and
activities according to virtue, which were also goods. The
virtues were regarded as necessary with regard to
happiness; joy and gladness were not necessary (3.113).

---

[21] J.C.B. Gosling and C.W.W. Taylor, *The Greeks on Pleasure* (Oxford, 1982)
417. For a comparison with Arist. *E.N.* 1174b31, see F.H. Sandbach, *Aristotle
and the Stoics. Cambridge Philological Society* Suppl.10 (1985) 27.
[22] A. von Fragstein, *Die Diaeresis bei Aristoteles* (Amsterdam, 1967) 81.
[23] *Concerning Emotions* 1 = SVF 3.391.

Diogenes Laertius refers to goods which are not always present, for example, joy and walking (3.102).[24] In Stobaeus, we find that every virtue and wise perception and wise impulse and similar things are real for all the wise and on every occasion, but that joy and gladness and wise walking are not real for all the wise or invariably (3.103). In a diaeresis of the goods, Stobaeus classifies joy, gladness and moderate association as 'things in movement' (*Ec.* II, p. 73,1-15 = 3.111).

If the movement of desire (*orexis*) towards that which ought to be desired (*orekteon*) is a movement towards 'something that gives pleasure to the extent that it should', then the movement of the impulse, 'choice (*hairesis*)' towards that which ought to be chosen (*haireteon*) is also a movement towards 'something that gives pleasure to the extent that it should'. We would expect that *hairetea*, such as 'thinking wisely' would be accompanied by or entail predicates which expressed emotions, such as, 'rejoicing (*chairein*)', or 'feeling glad (*euphrainesthai*)'. This is probably the case, although Stobaeus includes these two specifications for the emotions in a list of absolutely appropriate acts (3.501).

The pleasure that I have been discussing is obviously not the pleasure which is described in *Concerning Emotions*, the work of Ps.-Andronicus, an eclectic philosopher of the first century BC. He defines an emotion (*pathos*) as a movement of the soul, unaccountable (*alogos*), and contrary to nature, or an excessive impulse, and states that the generic emotions are four: pain, fear,

---

[24] We should notice a sentence in Seneca which reads: 'Not even joy (*gaudium*) which has its source in virtue, although it is good, is part of absolute good, no more than pleasure and tranquillity, although they arise from the first causes. For they are good, but supervene upon the highest good, and do not compose it' *De Vita Beata*, 15, 2). For a discussion of this sentence see M. Pohlenz, 'Philosophie und Erlebnis in Senecas Dialogen', *Nach. Ges. Wiss. Göttingen* 1, 4 (1941) 391-2.

appetite and pleasure (*hêdonê*).[25] He defines pleasure as an unaccountable elation (*alogos eparsis*) or a fresh *doxa* regarding the presence of good. Galen attributes the second definition of pleasure to Chrysippus,[26] and he adds another definition, namely that pleasure is 'an elation at what seems choiceworthy'.[27] I shall discuss these definitions in Chapter 9.[28]

The Stoics seems to have recognized three kinds of elation:

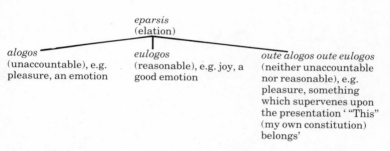

	eparsis (elation)	
alogos (unaccountable), e.g. pleasure, an emotion	*eulogos* (reasonable), e.g. joy, a good emotion	*oute alogos oute eulogos* (neither unaccountable nor reasonable), e.g. pleasure, something which supervenes upon the presentation ' "This" (my own constitution) belongs'

The threefold division of the diaeresis is well attested in our sources.[29]

The disinclination (*ekklisis*) is also classified as both 'unaccountable' and 'reasonable'. There are two kinds of disinclination: fear (*phobos*), an unaccountable disinclination (*ekklisis alogos*), which is defined as the avoidance of an expected danger (3.391), and precaution (*eulabeia*), a reasonable disinclination (*eulogos ekklisis*, 3.432). The disinclination accompanies the movement of the impulse. If it is in accord with the proposition to which the impulse gives assent, it is a reasonable disinclination; if it is not in accord, it is unaccountable. A movement of the impulse

[25] *Concerning Emotions* 6 = *SVF* 3.432. For the text of this work see *Pseudo-Andronicus de Rhodes, Peri pathon*, ed. A. Glibert-Thirry (Leiden, 1977).

[26] De Lacy, IV. 2.1-2.

[27] De Lacy, IV. 2.6.

[28] See pp. 129-30.

[29] Cf. Stob. *Ec.* II, p. 71,1-3.

away from that which ought to be reasonably desired might be accompanied by fear; and a movement towards that which ought to be reasonably desired might in some cases be accompanied by precaution. The latter disinclination would be consistent with the rational presentation: ' "This" (e.g. pain) is an indifferent.'

8

The Stoic *Telos*

In one of the most moving hymns of antiquity, Cleanthes prays to Zeus: 'Grant that I may find the judgment in which you trust and by which you steer all things with justice' (1.537,30-1).[1] What is this judgment for which Cleanthes prays? There is no doubt that the activity of the human soul paralleled the activity of Zeus. Zeus steers all things with law (2), guides the common *logos* which pervades all things (8-9), and harmonizes all good and evil so that there is one eternal *logos* of all things (16-17). Cleanthes speaks of the unfortunate who do not regard the common law of Zeus (20). If then the role of Cleanthes is similar to that of Zeus, Cleanthes is praying that he may have sufficient judgment to guide the *logos* within his soul, and by so doing regard the eternal *logos* of God.

In his *Concerning Law*, Chrysippus described the impulse (*hormê*) as a '*logos* prescriptive of action (*logos prostaktikos tou poiein*)' (3.175). It is also described as 'law prescriptive of what ought to be done and prohibitive of what ought not to be done' (3.314), and 'right *logos* prescriptive of what ought to be done and prohibitive of what ought not to be done' (Stob. *Ec*. II, p. 102,4-6).[2]

---

[1] For Cleanthes' *Hymn to Zeus* see particularly A.J. Festugière, *Personal Religion among the Greeks* (Berkeley, 1954) 5-12.

[2] For the *logos* that prescribes see R. Heinze, *Die Lehre vom Logos in der*

Chrysippus defined the *telos* (end of life) as: 'Living according to experience in those things that happen naturally (*to kat' empeirian tôn phusei sumbainontôn zên)*' (3.4). Long held that the words 'those things that happen naturally' refer to the 'preferreds', a class of the indifferents.[3] Zeno and Chrysippus recognized a class of 'indifferents' which included such terms as life, death, health, sickness, wealth and poverty, and they divided them into two groups, 'preferreds' and 'rejecteds', or 'things according to nature', and 'things contrary to nature'. Diogenes Laertius lists 'the preferreds' as life, health, pleasure, beauty, strength, wealth, a good reputation, and good birth (3.117). A little later he specifies them by wealth, a good reputation, health and strength (3.119). The Stoics described a 'preferred' as 'that which we select, although it is an indifferent, according to a directing *logos*' (3.128).

There is a very real possibility, however, that 'those things that happen naturally' are not a species of the indifferents, but the absolutely appropriate acts (*katorthômata*) towards which the *logos* that prescribes is moving. In a passage based on Chrysippus, and perhaps on his *Concerning Law*, Plutarch writes that the absolutely appropriate act is a prescription of law (*nomou prostagma*), and error a prohibition of law (3.520). If this sentence is studied in conjunction with the following passage in Stobaeus, it becomes clear that that which happens according to the right *logos* is the absolutely appropriate act:

---

griechischen Philosophie (Berlin, 1872, repr. 1984) 151, and nn. 2 and 3; A.A. Long, 'The Stoic concept of evil', *Philosophical Quarterly* 18 (1968) 334-9 and 342-3; and R. Pachet, 'L'impératif stoïcien', in *Les stoïciens et leur logique*, ed. J. Brunschwig (Paris, 1978) 361-74.

[3] A.A. Long, 'Carneades and the Stoic telos', *Phronesis* 12 (1967) 65. See also G. Striker, 'Antipater, or the art of living', in *The Norms of Nature*, ed. M. Schofield, G. Striker (Cambridge, 1986) 187-8, and A.M. Ioppolo, 'La dottrina Stoica dei beni esterni e i suoi rapporti con l'etica Aristotelica', *Rivista Critica di Storia della Filosofia* 29 (1974) 373-4.

That which is contrary to nature has been comprehended in our description of the affection, for it (sc. that which is contrary to nature) happens contrary to the right *logos* which is according to nature (*hôs sumbainontos para ton orthon kai kata phusin logon, Ec.* II, p. 89,14-16).[4]

'That which is according to nature' happens according to the right *logos* which is according to nature. 'That which happens according to the right *logos* which is according to nature' is the absolutely appropriate act. The verb 'happen' was used to describe a predicate or a proposition. Sextus Empiricus, for instance, defines the 'Good' as 'that according to which "being benefited" happens (*to kath' ho sumbainei ôpheleisthai*)' (*Math.* 11.26).

Posidonius, in an obvious paraphrase of Chrysippus' definition of the *telos*, writes:

> One cannot use the view (i.e. to resolve the difficulties posed by the sophists) that the end is 'to live according to experience in those things that happen according to the whole nature' which is equivalent to saying 'to live in agreement' (De Lacy, V.6.12).[5]

The words 'according to the whole nature' certainly suggest 'according to the prescriptive *logos*'. Zeno defined the *telos* as 'living in agreement (*to homologoumenôs zên*)' (1.179). In that case, 'living in agreement' was 'living in agreement with the prescriptive *logos*'. This is identical with 'living according to experience in those things that happen naturally', if indeed those things that happen naturally are the absolutely appropriate acts.

---

[4] On this passage see A. Graeser, *Zenon von Kition. Positionen und Probleme* (Berlin, 1975) 146.

[5] *SVF* 3.12. *Posidonius* 1. *The Fragments*, ed. L. Edelstein, I.G. Kidd (Cambridge, 1972) F 187.

Diogenes of Babylon's definition of the *telos* presents serious problems of interpretation: 'Acting rationally in the selection and rejection of those things that are according to nature (*eulogistein en têi tôn kata phusin eklogêi kai apeklogêi*)' (3.44). Görler in his recent article has drawn attention to a threefold division of 'things according to nature' attributed to Diogenes of Babylon:[6]

> All those things which are according to nature have value (*axia*), and all those things which are contrary to nature have no value (*apaxia*). Value is explained in three ways, (1) the evaluation (*dosis*) and estimate (*timê*) in itself, and (2) the assessment (*amoibê*) of the assessor (*Ec.* II, p. 83,10-13).

> The evaluation (*dosis*), Diogenes says, is a judgment regarding the extent to which it is according to nature, or the degree to which it provides some advantage naturally (II, p. 84,4-6) ... He says that these are the two values in accordance with which we say that some things are preferred in value, but he adds that there is a third in accordance with which we say that some things have worth (*axiôma*) and value. This value is not applicable to the 'indifferents' but to the goods alone. He says that we sometimes use the name, value, instead of 'that which is proper to', as we may understand from the definition of justice, when it is said to be 'a disposition capable of distributing that which is according to his value to each'. For it is, as it were, 'that which is proper to' each (*Ec.* II, p. 84,9-17).

The 'goods' to which the terms 'worthy' and 'value' may be applied are found in a diaeresis of the 'goods' in Stobaeus (*Ec.* II, p. 73,1-5):

---

[6] W. Görler, 'Zum Virtus-Fragment des Lucilius (1326-1338 Marx) und zur Geschichte der Stoischen Güterlehre', *Hermes* 112 (1984) 447-8.

```
                        ta agatha
                       (the goods)

ta en kinêsei                          ta en schesei
(those in movement,                    (those in condition, e.g.
e.g. joy, gladness,                    an orderly calm,
moderate association)                  unconfused
                                       persistence, manly
                                       diligence)

ta en hexei                            ta en schesei monon
(those in disposition,                 (those in condition
e.g. virtues, skills,                  only, as stated above).
pursuits)
```

More information is found in another diaeresis also in Stobaeus (*Ec.* II, p. 70,8-11 = 3.97):

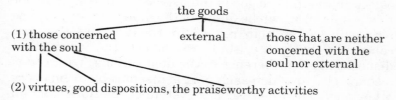

```
                         the goods

(1) those concerned       external        those that are neither
with the soul                             concerned with the
                                          soul nor external

(2) virtues, good dispositions, the praiseworthy activities
```

The second step in the diaeresis is repeated in the opening sentence in the next paragraph (*Ec.* II, p. 70,21-71,1 = 3.104):

(3) permanent dispositions, dispositions, neither dispositions nor permanent dispositions.

Stobaeus' source specifies the permanent dispositions by virtues, the dispositions by pursuits, and those that are neither dispositions nor permanent dispositions by 'activities according to virtue, such as, for example, wise conduct and the acquisition of moderation, and similar things' (p. 71,1-6). The last group seems to correspond to what was described earlier as 'praiseworthy activities'.

We should recall that Diogenes of Babylon defined his

telos as: 'Acting rationally in the selection and rejection of those things that are according to nature.' In what does this selection and rejection consist? If in Diogenes' definition 'those things that are according to nature' are the goods, we may paraphrase his definition to read: 'Acting rationally in the selection and rejection of the goods.' Is this a selection of those things that are according to nature and a rejection of their contraries? If this is the case, why did he not write simply: 'Acting rationally in the selection of those things that are according to nature'? In a sentence which appears to be a quotation from Antipater of Tarsus, Plutarch wrote: 'Let it be, as they themselves say, a rational selection of those things that have value for being happy' (*Comm. Not.* 1072D = *SVF* 3.59). Or is Diogenes referring to a selection among the goods themselves? Some support for this assumption can be found in the diaeresis. It would be wrong to say that in regard to 'those things that are concerned with the soul' we select the permanent dispositions in preference to the dispositions. The good is a composite in which each part is inseparable from every other part. The diaeresis is a system of relations, and an assessment of relative values. When we select, we select a good and make a statement, such as 'Virtue, a disposition, is a good', and reject the statement, 'Virtue, a condition, is good'.

This interpretation of Diogenes' *telos* is supported by the little we know about the meaning of the word *eulogistia* (reasonable calculation), the noun which corresponds to *eulogistein* (acting rationally) in the *telos*. It is defined in Stobaeus as: 'Exact knowledge capable of striking a balance and summing up what is due and what is paid' (3.264). Pseudo-Andronicus in his *Concerning Emotions* defined it simply as: 'Exact knowledge capable of summing up what is due and what is paid' (3.268). Both sources state that 'reasonable calculation' is a species of practical wisdom (*phronêsis*). Since exact knowledge (*epistêmê*) is an apprehension, reliable and made unchangeable by a *logos*, or a composite from such apprehensions (Stob. *Ec.* II, p. 73,19-74,3), a 'reasonable calculation' is an apprehension or a composite of such apprehensions which gives assent to an apprehensive presentation.

In *De Finibus* IV, Cicero offered three definitions of the Stoic *telos*. The first of these reads: 'To live in the continuous use of exact knowledge of those things that happen naturally' (*vivere adhibentem scientiam earum rerum quae natura evenirent, Fin.* IV.14 = 3.13). Cicero says that the definition was Zeno's, and that it was applicable to the wise man only. If Cicero is right in attributing it to Zeno, we may see how it formed the basis for both Chrysippus' and Diogenes' *telos*.

According to a passage in Stobaeus, Zeno defined the *telos* as 'living in agreement' (1.179), and Cleanthes as 'living in agreement with nature' (1.552, 3.12). Diogenes Laertius attributed the second definition to both Zeno and Cleanthes (1.552). For both of these philosophers the definitions 'living in agreement', and 'living in agreement with nature' were synonymous, for, as we have seen, the right *logos*, which is, of course, the prescriptive *logos*, is according to nature (*Ec.* II, p. 89,14-16). Again, according to Diogenes Laertius, Chrysippus believed that the nature in accordance with which we ought to live is both the common nature and the individual nature, although Cleanthes held that it was the common nature only (1.555). It is very unlikely that Cleanthes ever held the views attributed to him here.

In a very important passage, Cicero discusses the Stoic concept of *homologia* (agreement) and the 'highest good'. He writes that when a man sees 'the order and harmony of things to be done (*viditque rerum agendarum ordinem et ut ita dicam concordiam*)', he esteems them much more highly than all those things which he had loved first, and infers by reasoning that the highest good (*summum bonum*) of man depends on this (*in eo collocatum*).[7] He goes on to say that the highest good 'is assumed to depend (*positum sit in eo*)' on what the Stoics call *homologia* (*Fin*. 3.6.21). When a man sees 'the order and harmony of things to be done' (*homologia*), presumably he perceives the relation of the absolutely appropriate acts to one another, and their dependence upon the *logos* that prescribes. There is no reason to believe that *homologia* was a fixed disposition of the soul. Chrysippus' and Diogenes' definitions of the *telos* were consistent with Zeno's concept of *homologia*.

The Stoics held that only the 'fine (*kalon*)' was good (3.30 cf. 3.38). Since the Good includes virtue and that which participates in virtue, virtue and its participants are necessarily fine (3.30). Because the Good is 'naturally choiceworthy', the 'fine' is naturally choiceworthy (3.38, cf. 73). The exact meaning of the term 'fine' is difficult to determine. The most helpful definition is in Diogenes Laertius: 'Everything good is "fine" because it is in the right proportion with respect to its own function' (3.87).[8]

Like Diogenes, Antipater of Tarsus made a threefold classification of 'things according to nature'. There is nothing to suggest, however, that he recognized a class of 'things according to nature' which were goods.[9] It seems necessary, therefore, to assume that his first definition of the *telos*: 'To live selecting those things that are according to nature and rejecting those things that are contrary to nature' (3.57, p. 252) refers to the selection of the 'preferreds' out of the 'indifferents'.

'The preferred' is 'that which we select, although it is an indifferent, according to a directing *logos*' (3.128). The *logos* that selects seems to have formed the propositional

---

[7] See also T. Engberg-Pedersen, 'Discovering the good: *oikeiôsis* and *kathêkonta* in Stoic ethics', in *The Norms of Nature*, 156-72.

[8] For a discussion of the 'fine' see D. Tsekourakis, *Studies in the Terminology of Early Stoic Ethics. Hermes Einzelschriften* 32 (1974) 61-7; T.H. Irwin, 'Stoic and Aristotelian conceptions of happiness', in *The Norms of Nature*, 210-13.

[9] Cf. Stob. *Ec*. II, p. 83,13-84,3.

content of two presentations: ' "This" is an indifferent', and ' "This" is a preferred'. Such a presentation was a factor in determining the strength of the impulse, and whether it was excessive or in proportion. It was possible, however, for a man to give a weak assent to a presentation, such as ' "This" (i.e. pleasure) is an indifferent', and at the same time to move away from that which ought to be reasonably desired, or to give a weak assent to a *doxa*, such as ' "This" (i.e. pleasure) is a good', and to move towards that which ought to be reasonably desired. Antipater may have realized that a correct selection among the 'indifferents' was an important factor in the process of decision.

Plutarch attacked Antipater's first definition of the *telos* on the grounds that it was circular. The Stoics, Plutarch argued, select 'things according to nature' not because they are good, but because they have some value for acting rationally (*Comm. Not.* 1072E). Plutarch's objection seems valid, but whether these or similar objections motivated Antipater's decision to construct a second definition we do not know.

There is evidence for a heated exchange of views between Antipater and Carneades. Long referred to a passage in Cicero's *Academica* in which the question is asked: 'Why did Antipater fight with Carneades in so many volumes?'[10] Two observations offered by Carneades regarding the nature of the *telos* have been preserved:

> That with which practical wisdom is concerned and what it would like to attain ought to be something suited and adapted to our nature; it must be such that it can arouse and entice an impulse of the mind, which the Greeks call *hormê* (impulse, Cic. *Fin.* V.17).

> It is clear that no art is concerned only with itself, but the art is distinct from the object with which it deals (*Fin.* V.16).

[10] Long (1967) 76, n. 46.

Long argued that these or similar remarks led Antipater to abandon his first definition of the *telos* and construct the second;[11] the influence of Carneades on the second *telos* has also been recognized by Striker.[12]

Antipater's second definition read: 'Doing everything in one's power invariably and consistently with a view to attaining those things that lead the way (*ta proêgoumena*) according to nature' (3.57, pp. 252-3). The adverb *proêgoumenôs* was described by Dirlmeier on the basis of Stobaeus, *Ec.* II, p. 63,11-15, as 'an advance forward according to rank "in the first line" so that a second could follow after it'.[13] The *proêgoumena* are those things which lead the way as contrasted with those that are a result or consequence. The only evidence that we have for interpreting Antipater's second definition is a passage in Galen, based on Posidonius:

> Some, giving up 'living in agreement' reduce this to doing everything that is possible for the sake of those things that are primary according to nature, acting as if they were setting forth pleasure or freedom from trouble or some such thing as a goal (V.6.10 = *SVF* 3.12).[14]

Antipater's definition of the *telos* seems to be under attack. In Stoic philosophy, 'those things that are primary according to nature' referred to conditions of the

[11] ibid. 76-7; cf. O. Rieth, 'Über das Telos der Stoiker', *Hermes* 69 (1934) 31-4; R. Alpers-Gölz, *Der Begriff Skopos in der Stoa und seine Vorgeschichte* (Hildesheim, 1976) 71-3.

[12] Striker (1986) 189.

[13] F. Dirlmeier, 'Die *Oikeiôsis*-Lehre Theophrasts', *Philologus* Suppl. 30,1 (1937) 16.

[14] For this passage see Rieth (1934) 35-7, Long (1967) 80-3, Striker (1986) 193-4, Irwin (1986) 227 and n. 22. Görler (1984) 457, wrote: 'Bereits das legt die Vermutung nahe, dass in der Formel des Antipater nicht nur um die (sittlich indifferenten) *kata phusin* geht, die man, wenn sie bequem zur Verfügung stehen, "mitnimmt", sondern auch um wahre Werte oder *agatha*.'

body, such as health, soundness[15] and perception (3.141). What Posidonius is ridiculing, however, are states of mind, not conditions of the body. What kind of states of mind might be parodied by 'pleasure' or 'freedom from trouble'? Several might be suggested tentatively: the easy flow of life (*euroia biou*),[16] agreement (*homologia*) and happiness (*eudaimonia*).[17]

In his second definition, Antipater laid himself open to other charges. Plutarch, for instance, argued that the real end was 'the attaining of the primary things according to nature', and charged the Stoics with setting before us two ends and two goals. In a passage which includes, as Cherniss observed,[18] a 'conflation of the definitions formulated by Diogenes and Antipater', Plutarch writes:

It is to this that all actions must have their reference, to attaining the primary things according to nature (*Comm. Not.* 1071A) ... For (sc. they say) that the selecting and grasping of those things sensibly is an end, but that those things themselves and the attaining of them are not an end, but they are, as it were, some kind of matter which has selective value (1071B).[19]

---

[15] Stob. *Ec.* II, p. 82,11-15. Wachsmuth inferred *artiotês* (soundness) from *cheir artia* (a sound hand) on *Ec.* II, p. 82,17, and the inclusion of the term *artiotês* in the list of 'those things that are primary according to nature' on p. 47,23. For 'those things that are primary according to nature' see also *Ec.* II, p. 79,18-80,13 = 3.140.

[16] Irwin (1986) 227, pointed out that we do not know how the early Stoics used this term. Happiness is called an 'easy flow of life' (3.73).

[17] Happiness is 'the excellence of the soul' (3.57). Virtue was sufficient for happiness (3.49), and productive of happiness (3.53). Happiness was an internal goal, and 'attaining happiness (*to tuchein eudaimonias*)' or 'being happy (*to eudaimonein*)' was the *telos*.

[18] Plutarch *Moralia* XIII, Part II (Loeb, Harvard, 1976) 750, note a.

[19] For a discussion of this passage see M. Pohlenz, 'Plutarchs Schriften gegen die Stoiker', *Hermes* 74 (1939) 25-6; R. Philippson, 'Das Sittlichschöne bei Panaitios', *Philogogus* 85, N.F. 39 (1930) 360; Alpers-Gölz (1976) 85-7, 175, n. 376.

Antipater's second definition of the *telos* follows the pattern set by definitions of the stochastic craft (*stochastikê technê*). In this kind of craft the external result is something contingent which may not be realized in spite of the efforts of the man who is attempting to achieve it. Medicine was a stochastic craft. It was stochastic in that its task was to do everything in its power to produce health.

According to Plutarch, the *telos* in Antipater's second definition is the whole definition: 'Doing everything in one's power invariably and consistently with a view to attaining those things that lead the way according to nature' (3.57, pp. 252-3), and the goal (*skopos*) is 'attaining those things that lead the way according to nature'. In another definition of the *telos*, attributed to the followers of Chrysippus, the *telos* is 'to attain happiness (*to tuchein eudaimonias*)' and the goal is happiness (3.16). As Long wrote: 'Here we have no distinction between actions and their external object since happiness for the Stoics is an internal goal attained by virtuous behaviour.'[20]

Long, however, believed that the word *skopos* denoted the external result as well as the internal goal.[21] Irwin rejected this interpretation on the grounds that it would be inconsistent with the Stoic view that virtue is sufficient for happiness.[22] The difference between the two interpretations becomes clear in a much-discussed simile of an archer in Cicero's *De Finibus*:

> For if a man were to make it his purpose (*si cui propositum sit*) to take a true aim at something with a spear or arrow, just as we speak of an ultimate end in things which are good, his purpose would be to do everything he could to aim straight. The man in this

[20] Long (1967) 78.
[21] ibid. 79.
[22] Irwin (1986) 229, n. 25.

simile must do everything to aim straight, and yet, to do
everything to attain one's purpose, this, so to speak, is the
ultimate end, what we call the *summum bonum* in life,
but the actual hitting of the mark, to be sure, is that
which ought to be selected (*seligendum*), not that which
ought to be chosen (*expetendum, Fin.* 3.22).[23]

Long argues that Cicero uses the term *propositum* to
denote an external goal (*skopos*);[24] Irwin that he used it
to denote an external result, or objective.[25] The actual
hitting of the mark is not a *telos*, and Irwin seems to be
right in believing that it was not a goal either. The Greek
words translated by Cicero as *seligendum* and *expetendum* must surely be *eklekteon* (that which ought to be
selected) and *haireteon* (that which ought to be chosen).

In conclusion, I wish to say something about a very
puzzling passage in Diogenes Laertius which mentions
'the life according to nature':

> Of the indifferents they say that some things are
> preferred, others rejected: preferred are those that have
> value (*axia*), rejected are those that have no value
> (*apaxia*). They speak of the one value in connection with
> the life in agreement (*ton homologoumenon bion*), which
> is related to all good, and the other as some kind of
> intermediate power or function contributing to the
> natural life (*pros ton kata phusin bion*, 3.126).

Was there a 'natural life' separate and distinct from 'the
life in agreement'? If 'living according to nature' was
synonymous with 'living in agreement', why would not
the two descriptions of this life be identical in meaning?
Diogenes Laertius, however, is primarily concerned with

---

[23] For a discussion of the text of this passage see particularly O. Rieth (1934)
27-8; M. Soreth, 'Die zweite Telosformel des Antipater von Tarsos', *Arch. Ges.
Phil.* 50 (1968) 52-6; M. Pohlenz, 'Plutarchs Schriften gegen die Stoiker',
Hermes 74 (1939) 24, n. 4; Alpers-Gölz (1976) 75-80.

[24] Long (1967) 78-9.

[25] Irwin (1986) 230.

two kinds of value, the value that is related to the goods, and the value that is connected with the indifferents.[26] We may illustrate the 'life in agreement' as follows:

'This' (e.g. pleasure) is an indifferent.

'This' (absolutely appropriate act) ought to be chosen.

The two presentations would be followed by an act of assent, given by the impulse, to the proposition: 'It is reasonable that "this act" ought to be chosen', and by a movement of the rational impulse towards that which ought to be chosen. Concurrent with this movement is the movement of the impulse towards the *telos* 'living in agreement'. 'The life in agreement' is a disposition that follows upon the movement of the impulse towards the *telos*. In this example, the 'value' attached to the preferred is purely negative. Because the preferred is recognized as an indifferent, it does not distract the movement of the impulse away from those things which ought to be chosen.

To illustrate 'the life according to nature', or 'the natural life', I shall write:

'This' (e.g. pleasure) is an indifferent (i.e. preferred).

'This' (e.g. getting married) ought to be desired.

The two presentations would be followed by an act of assent to the proposition: 'It is reasonable that "this" (e.g. getting married) ought to be desired', and by a movement of the impulse towards that which ought to be desired (*orekteon*). 'That which ought to be desired', is synonymous with 'something that gives pleasure to the extent that it should (*epi ti<nos> hoson chrê hêdon<tos>*)'. Therefore, the movement of the impulse towards that which ought to be desired would be synony-

---

[26] For a discussion of value in early Stoic philosophy see Irwin (1986) 236-42. The source for these two kinds of value may be Diogenes of Babylon. See above, pp. 106-8.

mous with the movement of the impulse towards the *telos* 'to attain pleasure (*to tuchein hêdonês*), that is, 'to attain things according to nature (*to tuchein tôn kata phusin*)'. The 'natural life' is a condition that follows upon the movement of the impulse towards the *telos*. Here, the preferred, pleasure, plays a positive role. Along with the presentation ' "This" (e.g. getting married) is desirable', it helps to move the impulse towards that which ought to be desired, 'something that gives pleasure to the extent that it should'.

If, however, we substitute 'money' for 'pleasure' in the presentation of the indifferent, and 'serving as an ambassador' for 'getting married' in the presentation of the desirable, we receive a very different impression:

'This' (e.g. money) is an indifferent (i.e. preferred).	'This' (e.g. serving as an ambassador) ought to be desired.

In this case, money might, in fact, be a necessary condition for obtaining the position of ambassador, or fulfilling the duties required.

In Stoic philosophy, the movement of the *logos* that prescribes towards the *telos* does not exclude the movement of the impulse towards attaining 'things according to nature'. The life in agreement and the life according to nature were two aspects of the life of one human being at the same point in time.

9

The *Doxa*

What is the meaning of the term *doxa*? Stenzel considered the noun in relation to its verb *dokeô*, and argued that it had both an active and a passive meaning.[1] In its passive sense it should be translated as 'appearance', or 'reputation', the manner in which I appear; in an active sense, it is what appears to me, my opinion or judgment. Fränkel connected the older form *dokos* with *dechomai*, 'receive', or 'take up', and translated *dokei moi* as 'I take up an opinion or purpose'.[2]

The word *hupolêpsis* (assumption) in Aristotle has as its species exact knowledge, *doxa*, practical wisdom, and their contraries (*De Anima* 427b24-6). It is 'a general notion', a 'taking something to be the case', or 'an assumption'.[3] The passages that we have seem to indicate that the assumption was a general notion for the Stoics also. Chrysippus is quoted as saying in his *Concerning the Emotions* that avarice is an assumption that money is good and that drunkenness and indulgence should be regarded in the same way (3.456).

A sentence in Stobaeus suggests that the terms *doxa*

[1] J. Stenzel, 'Über den Einfluss der griechischen Sprache auf die philosophische Begriffsbildung', *N. Jb. f. Klass. Altertum* 47 (1921) 163.

[2] H. Fränkel, 'Xenophanesstudien', *Hermes* 60 (1925) 190. For *doxa* in Plato see Y. Lafrance, *La théorie platonicienne de la Doxa* (Montreal and Paris, 1981), and the review of this book by H. Cherniss, *Dialogue* 22 (1983) 137-62.

[3] M. Schofield, 'Aristotle on the imagination', in *Aristotle on Mind and the Senses*, ed. G.E.R. Lloyd, G.E.L. Owen (Cambridge, 1978) 125-9.

and assumption in Stoic philosophy were interchangeable: 'In the case of all the emotions of the soul, when
they say that they are *doxai*, the *doxa* is received in place
of (*anti*) the weak assumption' (*Ec*. II, p. 88,22-89,2).
Another passage, however, recognizes two kinds of *doxai*:

> Ignorance is an assent subject to change and weak. But
> the wise man does not make any assumption weakly
> (*hupolambanein asthenôs*), but rather firmly and stead-
> fastly, and because of this he does not form a belief either
> (*dio kai mêde doxazein*). For there are two *doxai*: the
> assent to a non-apprehensive, and the weak assumption
> (3.548).

It seems clear from the last sentence that the term *doxa*
denoted two separate acts: (a) the assent to the
non-apprehensive, and (b) the weak assumption. Tempo-
rally, (b) is prior to (a), since Stobaeus' source wrote: 'The
wise man does not make any assumption weakly, and
because of this (wherefore) he does not form a belief
either.'

The evidence for the non-apprehensive is found in
Diogenes Laertius:

> The non-apprehensive (*akatalêpton*) is (1) that which
> does not arise from a *huparchon* (that-which-is-real, *tên
> mê apo huparchontos*), or (2) that which arises from a
> *huparchon*, but is not according to the *huparchon* itself
> (2.53, p. 21).

In Chapter 6 I discussed the problems in the
interpretation of Diogenes' first definition.[4] Ostensibly,
'that which does not arise from a *huparchon*' includes all
presentations which are not apprehensive. It may,
however, designate only false presentations, such as 'The
oar in the water is broken'. The second definition

4 See pp. 79-81.

probably refers to a true and false presentation, such as 'Electra is a Fury'. These specifications are, of course, inadequate for any account of the Stoic process of decision. For the first kind of non-apprehensive I would suggest 'Pleasure is a good', and for the second 'The good is inexpedient'.

For further evidence I shall turn to two passages in a papyrus from Herculaneum:

> Because the wise man does not suppose (*doxazein*) anything, we say that several things result: first, that he does not suppose anything, for supposing (*dokêsis*) is a non-apprehensive belief; and that he does not conjecture anything, for conjecturing (*oiêsis*) is itself a belief (2.131, p. 40,21-5).

The term for 'supposing', explained as a non-apprehensive belief, corresponds to Stobaeus' definition of a belief as 'assent to a non-apprehensive', and the word for 'conjecturing' to Stobaeus' 'weak assumption' (3.548).

> For the wise man who disregards (*ton parorônta*) anything must receive a false presentation through sight, and accept it (2.131, p. 40,29-41,1).

The verb for 'accept' in the last line seems to imply 'giving assent to a false presentation'. There is every reason to believe that this is a belief (*doxa*).

In the passage that follows, lack of skill, disregarding, and cheating are listed together as intermediates (2.131, p. 41,17-18). If the last two required the giving of assent to a false presentation, the first term, lack of skill, may have done so also. If this is the case, a failure to be proficient in a particular instance is assent to a false presentation. This would appear to be an explanation for the Stoic assertions that the wise man was skilled in every craft (3.654,655).

The *doxa* as a true, rational presentation is described in a passage in Stobaeus:

> They say that there is a weak assent when we have not yet persuaded ourselves that this *doxa* is true, namely that we have five fingers, if it happens to be so, on each hand, and that twice two is four (3.172).

If the *doxa* gave assent to a true, rational presentation, it presumably gave assent to a true, perceptive presentation as well. For example, it gave assent to a presentation, such as 'It is day', when, in fact, day is present (2.65).[5]

The passage from Stobaeus quoted above specifically states that the wise man never makes a false assumption, and never gives assent to a non-apprehensive at all, and is not ignorant in any way (3.548). Ignorance, we are told, is an assent subject to change and weak (ibid.). If the wise man cannot give assent to a non-apprehensive, and the non-apprehensive can be specified by a true, perceptive presentation, such as 'It is day', when, in fact, it is day, then the wise man cannot give assent to a presentation of this kind. He cannot give assent to a true, rational presentation, such as 'Two plus two equals four', either. To preserve the freedom of the wise man to give assent to true presentations we have to assume that they were not *doxai*.

Arthur has drawn attention to a passage in Plutarch's *De Stoicorum Repugnantiis* (1056F = 2.993):

> They say that they err when they attach themselves to one (sc. of the presentations), instead of suspending judgment, that they are precipitate if they yield to what is not clear and are deceived if they yield to what is false,

[5] See pp. 51-2.

and are holders of belief (*doxazontas*) if they yield to what is commonly non-apprehensive.

There is certainly no reason to believe that *doxa* is a general term that covers both precipitation and self-deception, as Arthur seems to hold. Nor can we assume, as he does, that my inaccurate presentation of a square tower that appears to be round is a *doxa*.[6]

In many cases, where an apprehension is not possible, the wise man will suspend judgment. Cicero quotes the Stoics as saying that the wise man in a state of rage refrains from every assent because no distinction in visible objects is apparent (*Ac. Pr.* II.48 = 3.551). In addition to this, we have a passage in a papyrus which refers to *aproptôsia* (suspension of judgment) as a disposition on the basis of which one does not give assent to something before one has grasped it (*aproptôsia diathe(s)is asunkatathetos pro katalêpseôs*, *SVF* 2.131, p. 40,9-10).

In the case of false presentations, however, the error lay in giving assent to them:

'Again,' Chrysippus says, 'God makes false presentations and the wise man too, requiring us not to assent or yield to them, but only to act and direct our impulse towards the phenomenon, but we, in our folly, because of our weakness give assent to such presentations' (3.177).

He said that the wise man will cause harm by producing false presentations, if presentations are the sole cause of assents; for often wise men use (sc. something) false before those who are not wise and set forth a plausible presentation, yet not one that is a cause of the assent, since in that case it would be a cause of the false assumption and the deceit (2.994).

[6] E.P. Arthur, 'The Stoic analysis of the mind's reaction to presentations', *Hermes* III (1983) 73. See also Görler (1977) 88.

We may conclude, therefore, that the wise man withholds assent: (1) when an apprehension is not possible, (2) prior to the apprehension, when an apprehension is possible, (3) from a false presentation, or a true and false presentation.

The *doxa* gave assent to the non-apprehensive, that is, to a false presentation, or a true and false presentation. Like the apprehension, it was a species of assent (*sunkatathesis*), and the assent, in turn, was a part of the ruling part of the soul.

The judgment (*krisis*) should be identified with the *doxa*. The judgment that was capable of moving a violent and an excessive impulse was an emotion (3.384). The emotions, pleasure and pain, were fresh *doxai* (3.391, cf. 3.463). Posidonius distinguished the assumption from the *doxa*, and seems to have identified the judgment and the *doxa*:

> Posidonius tries to show the causes of all the false assumptions (*hupolêpseis*) in the theoretical <specu­lation arising through inadequate experience in the things that are, but in the practical> through the emotional pull, but the false beliefs (*doxai*) show the way for it, since the rational is weak in judgment (*peri tên krisin*).[7]

The Stoics described a judgment that was capable of moving a violent impulse and an excessive one as an emotion. There is no evidence that this was a specific judgment. A sentence in Galen states that 'sicknesses arise in the soul not simply because of a false assumption

[7] De Lacy V. 5.21. The lacuna in the text was filled by Pohlenz in the way that I have indicated, and his reconstruction was recently adopted by Theiler. Edelstein and Kidd (F 169) restored the lacuna to read: 'Speculation arising through ignorance, but in the practical.' See M. Pohlenz, *De Posidonii Libris Peri Pathon. Jahrb. f. Class. Philol.* suppl. 24 (1898) 560-2; M. Pohlenz, *Die Stoa*[4] 11 (Göttingen, 1949, 1972) 113; W. Theiler, *Poseidonios. Die Fragmente* I (Berlin and New York, 1982) 336; L. Edelstein and I.G. Kidd, *Posidonius 1. The Fragments* (Cambridge, 1972) F 169, p. 161.

about some things as good or evil, but because of believing them to be most important'. The passage concludes with the sentence: 'Arguing against the man who says this, Posidonius speaks as follows: "Such things were said by Chrysippus." '[8] 'Believing that money is the greatest good' may be followed by an impulse, an unaccountable desire (*alogos orexis* = *epithumia*), directed towards that which can be desired unaccountably (*epithumêteon*). If this is a desire for a specific sum of money, attainable by oneself, in excess of the amount reasonably desired, we may suppose that the judgment which moved the impulse was specific, for example, ' "This" (e.g. particular sum of money) is the greatest good'. The specification 'Pain is an evil' is attested in Cicero's *De Finibus* 3.29, and *Tusculan Disputations* 2.61. In the second passage, Posidonius is said to have cried out in the presence of Pompey: 'It is of no use, pain, no matter how much distress you cause me I shall never admit that you are an evil.' Pain in this sentence may be interpreted generically or specifically. If it is the particular instance of pain described by Posidonius, the *doxa* would read: ' "This" (particular instance of pain) is an evil.'

The *doxa* accounted for the excessive impulse, or the impulse that was disobedient to the *logos*. The latter is described in a much-discussed passage which reads:

> I think that something similar to this happens in the case of the impulses, because they exceed the due measure according to *logos* (*tên kata logon summetrian*), so that, when a man uses his impulse, he is not obedient to it (i.e. the *logos*). In the case of running, the excess is said to be over and above the impulse; in the case of the impulse, over and above the *logos* ... Therefore, when the transgression arises in this respect and in this way, it is

[8] De Lacy IV. 5.24-6.

said to be an excessive impulse and a movement of the soul, contrary to nature and unaccountable (*alogos*, IV.2.16-18).

In this passage, the relation of the *logos* to the impulse is analogous to the relation of the impulse to the running legs. The impulse is directing the running legs but it cannot bring the legs to a stop or change their pace. Its control over the legs is inadequate. Similarly, the *logos* does not have complete control over the excessive impulse. From this we may conclude that disobedience to the *logos* is disobedience to the present, ongoing activity of the *logos* that exercises choice. The excessive impulse cannot be viewed independently of the *logos* any more than the movement of the legs can be viewed independently of the impulse. The *logos* to which Chrysippus is referring is either the *logos* that exercises choice, that is, the logos that chooses to do appropriate acts, such as, respecting one's parents, brothers, and fatherland (3.495), or the *logos* that prescribes what ought to be done or prohibits what ought not to be done (3.314).

Plutarch is correct in explaining that the excess of the impulse is accompanied by a change in the emotions and the changes pertaining to a disposition or a fixed disposition:

> The same part of the soul, which they call the process of thinking (*dianoia*) and the ruling part of the soul, being completely altered and undergoing a change in the emotions and in the changes pertaining to a disposition or a fixed disposition, becomes vice and virtue, and has nothing unaccountable (*alogon*) in it; but it is called unaccountable when by excess of the impulse, after it has become strong and gained control, it is carried towards some absurdity contrary to the *logos* that exercises choice (3.459).

Since the judgment that was capable of moving a violent and an excessive impulse was an emotion (3.384), and the emotions, pleasure and pain, were fresh *doxai* (3.391, cf. 3.463), a change in the emotions was necessarily a change in the *doxa*. The change in the *doxai*, however, accompanied or was determined by a change in the disposition or the fixed disposition of the soul, for example, a change from the disposition self-control to lack of self-control, and from the fixed disposition courage to cowardice. The change in the *doxa* that occurred was a change from a *doxa*, such as 'Pain is an indifferent', to 'Pain is an evil'. The excess in the impulse arises when the *doxa* is altered, and the dispositions and fixed dispositions are changed. The ruling part, we are told, is carried towards some absurdity contrary to the *logos* that exercises choice, presumably towards 'that which can be unaccountably desired (*epithumêteon*)'.

Plutarch refers to the emotions as a 'bad *logos*': 'For the emotion is a *logos*, bad and undisciplined, arising from a bad and erring judgment, which has received additional intensity and strength' (3.459). Since the 'bad *logos*' has as its starting point a bad and erring judgment, it cannot be identified with the judgment. It must, therefore, be the movement of the impulse away from that which ought to be desired. Commenting on Ps.-Andronicus' definition of the emotion (3.391), Glibert-Thirry wrote:

La passion est un mouvement irrationel de l'âme et contraire à la nature, ou une inclination exagérée ... Mais cette même *hormê* est un mouvement du *logos* ... La passion est donc une opération du *logos* par laquelle il s'écarte de lui-même. Cette opposition de la raison à la raison est conçue comme une transformation intégrale du *logos* lui-même: le *logos* est appelé *alogos*, lorsqu'il est emporté hors de lui-même et entraîné à agir contrairement aux convictions de la droite raison.[9]

[9] A. Glibert-Thirry, 'La théorie de la passion chez Chrysippe et son évolution

That which acts contrary to right reason, however, is not the *logos*, but the impulse.

Ps.-Andronicus defines the emotion (*pathos*) as a movement of a soul, unaccountable (*alogos*) and contrary to nature, or an excessive impulse (3.391). Were the emotions, pain, pleasure, and fear, movements unaccountable and contrary to nature, but not impulses at all, or were these three emotions with the addition of appetite both unaccountable movements and excessive impulses? The latter appears to be correct. Chrysippus describes a movement of the rational animal, in which he is thrust forward in disobedience to the *logos*, and states that to this movement both definitions apply: 'the movement contrary to nature which arises thus unaccountably', and 'the excess in the impulses'. He adds: 'We must apprehend this "unaccountable (*alogon*)" as disobedient to the *logos* and turned aside with respect to the *logos*' (IV. 2.10-12). A little later, Chrysippus defines excess in the soul as an 'excessive impulse', and 'a movement of the soul contrary to nature, and unaccountable' (*alogos*, IV. 2.18). The two terms are used synonymously.

If Plutarch is right in accounting for vice and virtue in the soul by changes in the emotions and in the dispositions and fixed dispositions of the soul, we may show the connection between the emotions and the virtues as follows:

A

rational presentation	apprehensive presentation
'This' (e.g. pain) is an indifferent	'This' (e.g. act according to virtue) ought to be chosen.

chez Posidonius', *Revue philosophique de Louvain* 75 (1977) 410; cf. M. Forschner, 'Die Pervertierte Vernunft. Zur Stoischen Theorie der Affekte', *Philosophisches Jahrbuch* 87 (1980) 265-6.

The impulse gives assent to the proposition: 'It is reasonable that "this" ought to be chosen.' This is followed by the movement of the impulse towards that which ought to be chosen. The dispositions, as, for example, endurance and self-control, and the fixed dispositions, for example, courage and justice, follow the *logos* that exercises choice.

B

doxa	apprehensive presentation
'This' (e.g. pain) is an evil	'This' (e.g. act according to virtue) ought to be chosen.

The impulse gives assent to the proposition: 'It is reasonable that "this" ought to be chosen.' This is followed by the movement of the impulse away from that which ought to be chosen. This is the excessive impulse, disobedient to the *logos* that exercises choice.

The state of the ruling part of the soul is changed by the *doxa*, in conjunction with the depression or elation that follows upon the *doxa*, and the excessive impulse moved by the *doxa*. Because the *doxa*, and the excessive impulse are the emotion, the state of the ruling part is changed by the emotion. Since the virtues, as fixed dispositions, follow the *logos* that exercises choice, they are incompatible with the excessive impulse, which is disobedient to the *logos*. When a change occurs in the fixed disposition of the soul, the condition of the ruling part of the soul becomes 'vice'. Chrysippus repeatedly connects the virtues with the emotions.[10]

We can now understand why Chrysippus insisted that one ought not to yield to a false presentation (3.177, cf. 2.994). If the *doxa*, ' "This" (e.g. pain) is an evil', did not receive assent, it would not be followed by a contraction, and an excessive impulse contrary to the *logos* that

[10] De Lacy, VII. 1. 9, cf. V.5.40.

exercises choice. The *doxa*, both as a false or a true and false presentation, and as a species of assent to either presentation (3.548), had the power to deflect the impulse away from the *logos* that exercises choice. A recognition that 'things according to nature' and 'preferred' were indifferents, or what is called a correct choice among the indifferents was a prerequisite for the movement of the impulse according to the *logos* that exercises choice.

It is now clear why the Stoic wise man must be in a state of impassivity (*apatheia*). The wise man could not give assent to a *doxa*, experience a contraction, elation, or disinclination that followed upon a *doxa*, or an excessive impulse.[11]

Chrysippus defined pain (*lupê*) as a fresh *doxa* (*doxa prosphatos*) regarding the presence of evil, and pleasure as a fresh *doxa* regarding the presence of good (De Lacy IV. 2.1, cf. IV. 7.3-4). He also defined pain as a diminution (*meiôsis*) before what seems avoidable, and pleasure as an elation (*eparsis*) before what seems choiceworthy (IV. 2.5). Ps.-Andronicus makes a significant addition to the definitions of pain and pleasure when he writes: 'Pain is a contraction, unaccountable (*alogos*), or a fresh *doxa* regarding the presence of evil, at which they think that it is necessary for the contraction to occur'; and 'Pleasure is an elation, unaccountable (*alogos*), or a fresh *doxa* regarding the presence of good, at which they think that it is necessary for the elation to occur' (3.391).[12] The significance of the last phrase is emphasized in Galen:

[11] For further discussion of the *apatheia* see Glibert-Thirry, 395-7; N.P. White, 'Two Notes on Stoic Terminology', *AJP* 99 (1978) 118.

[12] *Concerning Emotions* 1 = *SVF* 3.391. Regarding these definitions of the emotions X. Kreuttner, *Andronici qui fertur libelli Peri Pathon. Pars Prior. De Affectibus* (Heidelberg, 1884) 42, wrote: *Andronicum religiosissime Chrysippi formas memoriae prodidisse censeo.* For a discussion of the emotions see R.P. Haynes, 'The theory of pleasure of the Old Stoa', *AJP* 83 (1962) 412-19; A. Graeser, *Zenon von Kition. Positionen und Probleme* (Berlin, 1975) 145-75; Glibert-Thirry (1977) 407-11; C. Gill, 'Did Chrysippus understand Medea?' *Phronesis* 28 (1983) 136-49; M. Frede, 'The Stoic Doctrine of the affections of

He says that the fresh (*to prosphaton*) is that which is near in time (*to hupoguion kata ton chronon*), but he requires that it should be explained to him why, when the *doxa* of evil is fresh, it causes the soul to contract and produces pain (IV. 7.4).

Even if, as Theiler[13] and De Lacy believed, the word *phêsi* (he says) in this passage refers to Posidonius, it seems clear that Chrysippus held that a fresh *doxa* regarding the presence of evil caused the soul to contract. A sentence in Stobaeus states that *to prosphaton* was a term used 'instead of a contraction, unaccountable (*alogos*), capable of arousing movement' (*Ec.* II, p. 89,2-3).[14]

Galen quotes a long and important passage from Chrysippus regarding the relaxation of pain:

'One might investigate regarding the relaxation of pain, how it comes about, whether it comes about when some *doxa* is changed, or when all remain constant, and why this will be.' Then he adds: 'It seems to me that such a *doxa* remains, that that which is present is evil, but, when it persists in time, the contraction is relaxed, and, I believe, the impulse that follows upon the contraction. Even if this remains (*tautês diamenousês*), what follows will not heed it, because of some other disposition of a certain kind, not easily understood, which supervenes, when these things happen (*dia poian allên epiginomenên diathesin dussulogiston toutôn ginomenôn*)' (IV. 7.13-16).

In this passage, I have followed De Lacy in translating *hê epi tên sustolên hormê* as 'the impulse that follows on the contraction', rather than 'impulse to the contraction', as

---

the soul', in *The Norms of Nature*, ed. M. Schofield, G. Striker (Cambridge, 1986) 93-110; J.C.B. Gosling and C.C.W. Taylor, *The Greeks on Pleasure* (Oxford, 1982) 415-27.

13 Theiler (1982) II, p. 354, F 410.

14 For 'fresh' (*prosphatos*) see Forschner, 262-3.

was suggested by Inwood.[15] It is clear from another passage in Galen that the contraction followed the *doxa*:

> Chrysippus in the first book of his *Concerning Emotions* tries to show that the emotions are certain judgments of the rational part of the soul. Zeno thought that they were not the judgments themselves, but that the contractions and expansions, the elations and depressions of the soul that follow upon these, were the emotions (V. 1.4-5 = 3.461).

If further confirmation is needed, we find it in a quotation from Chrysippus recorded by Plutarch. After saying that anger intercepts 'those things that are being apprehended', Chrysippus writes that 'the emotions which supervene drive out the reasonings and those things that appear otherwise' (3.390). The emotions supervene upon the *doxai*, and drive out the apprehensive presentations.

There are, of course, problems in the interpretation of the earlier passage. First, what is it that remains? Is it the impulse, as De Lacy and Theiler suggested?[16] Galen obviously assumed that the *doxa* remained, for he wrote a few lines later: 'That in time the emotions cease, although the *doxa* remains, Chrysippus himself admits' (IV. 7.18). To illustrate a situation in which the *doxa*, the contraction, and the impulse remain strong I shall write:

'This' (e.g. pain) is an evil (*doxa*), followed by a contraction (i.e. pain).	'This' (appropriate act) ought to be reasonably desired.

The impulse gives assent to the proposition: 'It is reasonable that "this" (appropriate act) ought to be reasonably desired.' This is followed by a movement of

---

[15] B. Inwood, *Ethics and Human Action in Early Stoicism* (Oxford, 1985) 151.

[16] De Lacy IV. 7.10, Theiler (1982) II, p. 354, F 410.

the impulse away from that which ought to be reasonably desired.

If we assume that the words *tautês diamenousês* (even if this remains) refer to the *doxa*, then the phrase means: 'Even if this (i.e. the *doxa*) remains, that which follows (i.e. the contraction and the movement of the impulse) will not heed it.' In other words: 'Even if this (i.e. the *doxa*) remains, the impulse will not move away from that which ought to be reasonably desired.' 'What follows' will not heed the *doxa* because of a certain kind of disposition. This disposition may be exact knowledge, or more specifically in this instance, courage, exact knowledge regarding what should inspire confidence and what should not. Because of this disposition of the soul, the impulse does not heed the *doxa*.

If, however, the impulse does move away from that which ought to be reasonably desired, we have to assume not only a strong *doxa* and a strong contraction, but a state of ignorance in the soul, which has no power to resist the movement of the impulse away from that which ought to be reasonably desired.

This interpretation is supported by a passage in Chrysippus' *Concerning Inconsistency*:

'Anger is blind and often does not allow us to see what is apparent but often intercepts those things that are being apprehended (*ta katalambanomena*)', and a little later he says: 'For the emotions which supervene (*ta gar epigignomena pathê*) drive out the reasonings and those things that appear otherwise, violently pushing us forward to the contrary activities' (3.390).

The words 'those things that are being apprehended' refer to an apprehensive presentation, such as, ' "This" (i.e. the appropriate act) is reasonably desirable'. The apprehensive presentation receives assent from an apprehension (*katalêpsis*) or the composite of apprehensions which compose a cardinal virtue, such as, for example, 'courage (*andreia*)'. 'The emotions that supervene' are the contractions and expansions that supervene upon the *doxai*, and 'those things which appear otherwise' are again the apprehensive presentation. We may illustrate this as follows:

'This' (e.g. that of which I am being deprived) is good, a *doxa*, followed by a contraction (i.e. anger).	'This' (i.e. appropriate act) ought to be reasonably desired.

The impulse gives assent to the proposition: 'It is reasonable that "this" (appropriate act) ought to be reasonably desired.' This is followed by a movement of the impulse away from that which ought to be reasonably desired. The state of the soul is ignorance.

How, then, can we interpret Chrysippus' statement, if the words *tautês diamenousês* (even if this remains) refer to the impulse (IV.7.15-16)? Can the *doxa* and the contraction be relaxed while the impulse remains the same? Presumably they can until the *doxa* and the contraction become so weak that they no longer direct the movement of the impulse away from that which ought to be reasonably desired. If, however, the *doxa*, the contraction, and the movement of the impulse are essentially in accord, the soul must be in a state of ignorance. How then could 'what follows' fail to heed? I find it impossible to reconstruct this passage if indeed these words refer to the impulse.

In my reconstruction of the emotion, pain, I have argued that the impulse moves away from that which ought to be reasonably desired. For the emotion pleasure we may conjecture that the impulse moves away from that which ought to be reasonably desired, and towards that which can be desired unaccountably (*epithumêteon*). The emotion 'appetite' (*epithumia*) is defined as 'unaccountable desire' (*alogos orexis*), or the pursuit of an expected good (3.391).

The *doxa* is in a constant state of flux, and is progressively strengthened or weakened. The variation in the strength of the *doxa* is followed by a contracting or relaxing. The impulse suffers a change in degree. Although the state of the *doxa* is sufficient to explain vacillation and indecision, strong, conflicting emotions have to be explained in terms of conflicting *doxai*, or contrary presentations. The one who experienced the conflicting emotions substituted one *doxa* for another in rapid succession:

> Some say that the emotion is not different from the *logos* and that there is not any difference or dissension between the two, but it is a turning of one *logos* in both directions, but we do not notice this because of the quickness and the speed of the change (3.459).

The ruling part of the soul in this situation substitutes one *doxa* for another, or one presentation for another.

Chrysippus seems to have been particularly interested in explaining why a man who knows that what he is about to do is evil nevertheless determines that it must be done. He paid particular attention to two lines in Euripides' *Medea* (De Lacy III. 3.16-17).

> I understand the evils I am about to do,
> but my anger (*thumos*) is stronger than my counsels (1078-9).[17]

Galen believed that Chrysippus quoted these lines most inappropriately, arguing that they supported the theory of a tripartite division of the soul (III. 3.15-22, cf. IV. 6.19-20). He emphasized that Medea acted with full knowledge of the magnitude of the evil she was going to do, and spoke of her vacillation between anger and reason.

---

[17] For a discussion of these lines see Gill (1983) 136-49.

One particular quotation which Galen introduces in the context of the *Medea* is especially significant:

> Therefore, we can hear such words in the case of lovers and those who experience other violent, irrational desires, and those who are angry: that they wish to gratify their anger (*thumos*),[18] and to let them go, whether it is better or not, and to speak nothing to them, and that this ought to be done by all means, even if they err (*diamartanousi*), and if it is inexpedient (*asumphoron*) for them (IV. 6.27).

We find in the text of the *Medea* two antithetical *doxai*: 'To be cared for by one's children in one's old age is good' (1033), and 'To be laughed at by one's enemies is evil' (1049-50). The failure of Medea to recognize both of these as indifferents constituted an intellectual error. Medea has an apprehensive presentation: 'To protect the life of my child is choiceworthy.' Because protecting the life of her child was choiceworthy, it was good and expedient; killing her own child was, therefore, evil and inexpedient. The presentation, 'Killing my child is good', is a *doxa*, and the contrary of the presentation 'To protect the life of my child is choiceworthy', and it has never received assent. It seems, therefore, that the *doxa*, 'To be laughed at by one's enemies is evil', is a judgment which has moved the impulse towards an act which should have its source in another judgment which has not received assent. Although, of course, there is no direct evidence for Chrysippus' interpretation of the *Medea*, we may safely assume that he discussed her murder of her children in terms of conflicting *doxai*.

In conclusion, I shall provide a summary of my difficult exposition. The word *doxa* denoted both a weak assumption and assent to an non-apprehensive, that is,

---

[18] For the meaning of *thumos* see A. Dihle, *The Theory of Will in Classical Antiquity* (California, 1982) 26-7.

assent to a false or a true and false presentation. The *doxa* was a judgment, and a judgment that was capable of moving a violent and excessive impulse was an emotion. A change in the *doxa*, for instance, from 'pain is an indifferent', to 'pain is an evil', was accompanied by a change in the disposition or the fixed disposition of the soul, for example, from self-control to lack of self-control, and from courage to cowardice. The excess in the impulse arises when the *doxa* is altered and the disposition and the fixed disposition are changed.

The state of the ruling part of the soul is changed by the *doxa*, in conjunction with the depression or elation that follows upon the *doxa*, and the excessive impulse moved by the *doxa*. Since the *doxa*, the elation or depression, and the excessive impulse are the emotions, the state of the ruling part is changed by the emotions. Chrysippus repeatedly connects the virtues, the condition of the ruling part of the soul, with the emotions. There are varying degrees in the strength of the *doxai*, and the elations and depressions of the soul, and, more importantly, there are degrees in the strength and weakness of the soul which prevent or fail to prevent the movement of the impulse away from that which ought to be reasonably desired. Conflicting emotions must be explained by conflicting *doxai*.

10

The Parts and Dispositions of the Soul

The Greek word *hêgemonikon* should be translated as 'that which is capable of ruling or guiding'. It is the ruling part of the soul. It should not be translated as mind or reason, although it is something identified with *dianoia* 'thinking', or 'the process of thinking' (1.202, 3.306).[1] Although it is found only in its adjectival form in Plato and Aristotle,[2] it obviously has some affinities with the *pneuma*, situated in the heart, which is recognized as the source of movement in Aristotle's *De Motu Animalium* (703a10-19).[3] Since the term was used to describe the ruling part of the human soul, it served to emphasize the unity between the world soul and the soul of man (2.644).

I shall begin this chapter by examining a passage in Galen whose significance seems to have been overlooked:

> But if you believe that each of the concepts and anticipations is a part of the soul, you err for two reasons. First, you should not have said that these were the parts of a soul but parts of a *logos*, just as you write in your

[1] E. Asmis, *Epicurus' Scientific Method* (Ithaca, N.Y., 1984) 105-6.

[2] F. Adorno, 'Sul Significato del Termine Hegemonikon in Zenone Stoico', *La Parola del Passato. Rivista di Studi Classici* 14 (1959) 29. The evidence for the use of the term *hêgemonikon* in the fifth century BC is very poor. The adjectival form *hêgemonikos*, however, was used by Plato to describe the soul in *Phaedrus* 252E, exact knowledge in *Protagoras* 352B, and the handicrafts in *Philebus* 55D. The ending *-ikos* is found frequently in Aristotle.

[3] M.C. Nussbaum, *Aristotle's De Motu Animalium* (Princeton, 1978) 51, 145, 160.

investigation *Concerning a Logos*. For, I suppose, a soul and a *logos* are not the same ... Do not then confuse the parts of the soul with the activities. The concepts and anticipations are activities (*energeiai*) <but parts> of the soul, as you yourself teach in other passages, are the *pneuma* for hearing and seeing, and, in addition, the *pneuma* for speaking and reproduction, and above all, the ruling part of the soul, in which you said that the *logos* was constituted (De Lacy V.3.2-3, and 7).

In the last sentence, von Arnim wrote: *energeiai <moria> de tês psuchês*, and he was followed in this by De Lacy.

For reasons which will become clear later in the discussion we cannot assume that Galen was correct in inferring that Chrysippus held that the concepts and anticipations were parts of the soul. This is simply Galen's misinterpretation of a previous quotation from Chrysippus (V.2.49). We can, however, accept his statement that Chrysippus held that each of the concepts and anticipations was a part of a *logos*. Galen is arguing that each of the concepts and anticipations was a part of a *logos*, but not a part of a soul, but rather it is an activity of the soul.

If the ruling part of the soul was a part of the soul, and the concepts and anticipations were parts of the *logos*, it is reasonable to suppose that the *logos* was a part of the ruling part of the soul and write:

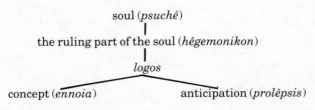

soul (*psuchê*)

the ruling part of the soul (*hêgemonikon*)

logos

concept (*ennoia*)   anticipation (*prolêpsis*)

If the Stoics described the terms of their diaeresis as parts, they had a precedent in Plato. In the *Sophist*, Plato refers to a division into parts, such as footed game or swimming game (221E2-3, cf. 220B9-10).[4] Plato's purpose in constructing a diaeresis was to define a species by a list of differentiae, such as, for example, 'Man is an animal, biped, wingless'. This led, however, to an exhaustive classification of a species.[5] The Stoics rejected the division of a genus by its differentiae as an adequate method of classification. In doing so, they may have been influenced by the attacks on this method that were made by members of the early Academy. The Stoic diaeresis represented substrata. Each term in the diaeresis was formed from the preceding term and an essential characteristic (*idion*), and consequently, each term in the diaeresis was more highly differentiated than the preceding one.[6]

Inwood, in .his recent discussion of the 'power' (*dunamis*) of the soul, argued on the basis of a passage in Iamblichus that the soul had four powers, presentation, assent, impulse and *logos* (2.826).[7] In doing so, he took issue with Pohlenz, who had argued in his *Zenon und Chrysipp* that the soul had only one power.[8] The question is important, and I propose to reopen it again. Several passages in Galen refer to Chrysippus' position that there was only one power of the soul:

> Chrysippus errs greatly, not because he made no virtue a power ... but because, although he said that there were many instances of exact knowledge and virtue, he

---

[4] For the Platonic diaeresis see J.M.E. Moravcsik, 'Plato's method of division', in *Patterns in Plato's Thought* (Boston, 1973) 163.

[5] See D.M. Balme, 'Aristotle's use of differentiae in zoology', in *Articles on Aristotle 1. Science*, ed. J. Barnes, M. Schofield, R. Sorabji (London, 1975) 183.

[6] For the Stoic diaeresis see O. Rieth, *Grundbegriffe der Stoischen Ethik* (Berlin, 1933) 45-51.

[7] B. Inwood, *Ethics and Human Action in Early Stoicism* (Oxford, 1985) 30-7.

[8] M. Pohlenz, 'Zenon und Chrysipp', *Nach. Ges. Wiss. Göttingen Phil.-hist. Kl. N.F. 2*, 9 (1938) 185, 210.

maintained that there was only one power (*dunamis*) of the soul (V. 5.38-9).

> The man who assumed that there was one power in the soul, called rational and critical ... just as Chrysippus did (VII. 1.13).

Pohlenz drew attention to a passage in Alexander: 'The power (*dunamis*) of the soul, being single, is such that the same (power), being in a certain disposition, at times shows purpose, at times becomes angry, and at times desires unaccountably' (2.823).[9] Sextus Empiricus wrote that the same power is in one respect *nous* (intellect) and in another *aisthêsis* (perception, 2.849). In spite of its similarity to passages in the *Nicomachean Ethics* and the *De Anima*, the statement is probably Stoic.[10] The one power of the soul effects many activities in accordance with the parts of the soul. The soul as a power effected the activity of anticipating (*prolambanein*). The 'anticipation', however, was not an activity of the soul, but as Chrysippus stated, a part of a *logos* (De Lacy V. 3.2).

There seems to be very little difference between 'the power of thinking' and 'the activity of thinking', if we remember that the Stoics used the word 'power' to denote the actual rather than the potential. To say, therefore, as Galen did (De Lacy V. 3.2-3), that the anticipation is an activity of the soul seems to entail that the anticipation is a power of the soul. Since Chrysippus recognized only one power of the soul, he could not have regarded the anticipation as an activity of the soul.

There are, however, passages which name parts of the soul as powers. Of these the most important and controversial are found in Iamblichus:

> And what is more, the followers of Chrysippus and Zeno

---

[9] ibid. 185.
[10] See A.-J. Voelke, *L'idée de volonté dans le stoïcisme* (Paris, 1973) 21, n. 3.

and all who conceive the soul as corporeal bring together powers (*dunameis*) as qualities in the substratum, and they postulate the soul as a substance underlying the powers, and they form a composite nature from both of these, although they are dissimilar (2.826).

Some (sc. powers) by the individuality of their quality in the same substratum, for just as the apple has in the same body sweetness and fragrance, so the ruling part of the soul possesses in the same body presentation (*phantasia*), assent (*sunkatathesis*) impulse (*hormê*), and *logos* (2.826).[11]

It is clear that Iamblichus recognizes four powers of the soul. Although these powers are not indistinguishable, each power can function only in relation to the other three. They owe their existence to the substance in which they inhere and they are expressions of that substance. This passage, in my opinion, does not represent the psychology of Chrysippus. It directly contradicts Chrysippus' statements, as they are reported in Galen, that the soul had only one power. Further, since Chrysippus held that the *logos* was a part of the soul, he certainly could not have considered it to be an individual quality, a term that he applied to the virtues (3.255). It would be wrong to assume that those Stoics who regarded the parts of the soul as powers recognized only four powers, for Aetius wrote:

The Stoics say that the ruling part is the highest part of the soul, that which produces the presentations, assents, perceptions and impulses, and this they call 'reasoning' (2.836).

[11] Philippson accepted the statement of Iamblichus and wrote: 'Diese *dunameis* des *hêgemonikon* sind also durch verschiedene Beschaffenheit von einander getrennt ... die *hormê* muss eine Eigenschaft haben, die sie vom *logos* unterscheidet.' R. Philippson, 'Zur Psychologie der Stoa', *Rh. Mus.* N.F. 86 (1937) 156. Voelke, however, believed that the passage was too vague to provide significant evidence: Voelke (1973) 21. Recently, Long argued in favour

It is not clear from this passage whether the ruling part is said to produce powers or parts.

Simplicius defines a power (*dunamis*) as that which is 'capable of bringing about several occurrences, and controlling the subordinate activities'. Unfortunately, he specifies the power by the virtue 'practical wisdom (*phronêsis*)' and the occurrences by 'walking sensibly' and 'discoursing sensibly' (3.203). For Chrysippus at least, the virtue, practical wisdom, was a cause of the attribute and predicate, but not a power (cf. 1.89). Last of all, I would draw attention to a sentence in Aetius: 'the term *aisthêsis* is used in many ways, the disposition (*hexis*), and the power (*dunamis*), and the activity' (*energeia*, Diels, *Dox. Gr.* IV. 8.1). Since the passage uses the Aristotelian term 'sense organ', it may not be early Stoic.

The Stoic 'parts of the soul' bear little resemblance to the Aristotelian faculties.[12] Commenting on *De Anima* 424a17, Hamlyn wrote: 'In this passage Aristotle is saying that the faculty is the organ's capacity for functioning, so that the organ cannot be physically distinguished from the faculty.'[13]This definition simply does not apply to the Stoic 'parts'. The ruling part of the soul was not an organ, and it would not be true to say that the presentation cannot be distinguished from the ruling part of the soul.

Statements which attribute to the early Stoics irrational powers should be regarded with some scepticism. When Posidonius attempted to prove that Cleanthes recognized three powers, the desiderative, the spirited, and the rational (1.571), he was merely trying to find support for his own tripartite division of the soul.

---

of the authenticity of the passage: A.A. Long, 'Soul and body in Stoicism', *Phronesis* 27 (1982) 49-50. See also Inwood (1985) 30-1.

[12] D.W. Hamlyn, 'Aristotle's account of *aesthêsis* in the *De Anima*', *CQ* 9 (1959) 10.

[13] ibid.

Galen claims that Chrysippus recognized a desiderative and a spirited power in his *Concerning the Soul*. He states, however, that in *Concerning the Affections* he wrote ambiguously at times, and at other times as if he believed that the soul had neither a desiderative nor a spirited power (3.461).

Chrysippus argued that those who were not wise had a sickness in their soul. This 'sickness of the soul' resembles 'a sickly bad disposition of the body (*têi nosôdei kachexiâi tou sômatos*) in accordance with which it gives way and falls into irregular, non-periodic fevers' (V. 2.7).[14] This quotation, which comes from Posidonius, is paraphrased several times by Galen (V. 2.31, V. 2.43, V. 3.12).

Galen believes that Chrysippus was not able to demonstrate what he had promised in his *Therapy of Ethics*, namely, 'the proportion <and disproportion> of the soul's parts to one another with regard to which the soul is said to be healthy and sick' (V. 2. 43-4). It is not at all clear whether the words 'with regard to which the soul is said to be healthy and sick' is part of what Chrysippus had promised to demonstrate. We do know, however, that a soul was called beautiful or ugly if it had or did not have such a proportion:

Therefore, a soul will also be called beautiful or ugly in proportion, according to the proportion or disproportion of some parts (V. 2.47).

Galen insists that Chrysippus did not say what these parts were (V. 2.48), and he goes on to quote a sentence in Chrysippus with no understanding of its context:

[14] W. Theiler, *Poseidonios. Die Fragmente* II F 413 (Berlin and New York, 1982).

There are parts of the soul by means of which (*di' hôn*) the *logos* in it (*en autêi*, the soul) and the fixed disposition in it (*en autôi*) are established (*sunestêke*). And a soul is beautiful or ugly according to the ruling part; for it is <such> or such according to its proper divisions (V. 2.49).

There are several problems in the interpretation of this sentence. The first is the meaning of *di' hôn*. Liddell and Scott mentions an instrumental use of *dia*, 'by', or 'by means of', which seems preferable here. The phrase 'the fixed disposition in it' cannot refer to 'the fixed disposition in the *logos*', since the *logos* certainly did not have a fixed disposition, but rather to the 'fixed disposition of the ruling part of the soul'.

Galen is confused about the proper divisions of the soul when he quotes the first part of the sentence above: 'There are parts of the soul by means of which the *logos* is established' (V. 3.1). He goes on to infer that the parts of the soul to which Chrysippus is referring are the concepts and anticipations. His interpretation is a red herring. Chrysippus is not talking about the parts which compose or make up the *logos*, but rather about the parts of the soul by which the *logos* is established. The Greek word *sunestêke* may mean either 'is proved', 'is established', 'is put together', or 'is composed'. The *logos* and the fixed disposition in the ruling part of the soul are established by the parts of the soul. We have already seen that the formation of the *logos* depended upon the presentation, the assent to the presentation and the proposition, and the impulse. The presentation, the assent, and the impulse, three of Iamblichus' powers (2.826), were, I believe, the parts of the soul by which the *logos* is established. If this is correct, we may write:

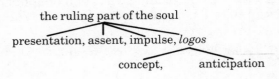

If, however, these three parts establish the *logos*, they also establish the disposition and the fixed disposition of the soul, since, as I have argued, they are capable of following the *logos* that exercises choice (3.384).

The *logos*, however, is not only established by other parts of the soul, but it itself establishes the proportion of the impulse. 'The proportion of the natural impulse' is 'the proportion according to the *logos*' (IV. 2.18). When the transgression occurs, the impulse is said to be excessive, contrary to nature and an unaccountable (*alogos*) movement of the soul (IV. 2.18). On the contrary, an impulse may be said to be according to nature and obedient to the *logos* when it does not exceed the proportion of the *logos*.

When all the parts of the soul are functioning according to the proportion of the *logos*, and when the disposition and fixed disposition follow the *logos* that exercises choice, the soul is in a state of tension (*eutonia*) and strength (*ischus*, IV. 6.2). This, however, is not always the case. What happens when the *doxa*, accompanied by a contraction or elation, controls the impulse and causes it to move in disobedience to the *logos*? The condition of the soul is no longer able to function. It gives in (IV. 6.6). There is a 'state of relaxed tension (*atonia*)' and weakness (IV. 6.1). Chrysippus describes this condition of the soul when he writes:

> One man withdraws when fears assail him, another becomes weak when profit or punishment appears and gives in, another for many other such reasons. Every such experience overturns and enslaves us so that, by giving in to them, we betray our friends and our cities, and we give ourselves up to many shameless deeds, because our former impulse (*phora*) has been relaxed. Menelaus was introduced as such a person by Euripides (IV. 6.7-9).

It is particularly significant that the Stoics identified the *tonos* with quality. Plutarch says that 'the qualities, being *pneumata*, and airy tensions (*tonous aerôdeis*), give form and shape to the several things, in whatever parts of matter they happen to be' (2.449). The 'state of relaxed tension (*atonia*)' brings about the destruction of the individual quality. A cardinal virtue, as we have seen, was an individual quality.[15]

Although we may with some confidence assume that Chrysippus adopted a concept of 'sympathy' in explaining 'how the divine *pneuma* so penetrates the cosmos as to keep the whole and its parts ... in a state of *tonos*, which produces unity and coherence',[16] the evidence has been challenged. Graeser mentions three passages to support his belief that Chrysippus used the concept: Alexander of Aphrodisias *De Mixtione* 216, 14 (*SVF* 2.473), Cicero *De Fato* 7 (2.950), and Ps.-Plutarch *De Fato* 574E (2.912). The passage in Alexander begins with the words: 'This is the belief of Chrysippus concerning mixture', and goes on to say:

> He assumes that the whole substance is unified, for a *pneuma* permeates through all of it, and by this the all is bound together, remains together, and is 'in sympathy' with itself.

Theiler argued that these words should not be attributed to the early Stoics, because there are similarities between them and sentences assigned to Posidonius.[17] Theiler's arguments, however, are not conclusive. I do not believe that there are sufficient grounds for rejecting the attribution to Chrysippus.

In a passage based on Chrysippus, Cicero speaks *de ipsa contagione rerum* (2.950). The word *contagio* is the word that Cicero normally uses to translate the Greek

[15] For 'tension' see M. Pohlenz, *Die Stoa*[4] (Göttingen, 1947, 1970) 74-5; D.E. Hahm, *The Origins of Stoic Cosmology* (Ohio, 1977) 169-73.

[16] A. Graeser, *Plotinus and the Stoics* (Leiden, 1972) 69.

[17] Theiler (1982) II, p. 151.

sumpatheia. This would seem to indicate that Chrysippus himself discussed 'sympathy'. Finally, we have a sentence in Ps.-Plutarch's *De Fato* (574E = 2.912) which reads: 'That this cosmos is organized by nature, since it shares in a common *pneuma* and is sympathetic with itself (*sumpnoun kai sumpathê auton autôi onta*).'[18] The passage is based on Chrysippus.

Through 'sympathy' the *logos* of the individual was united with the *logos* of the cosmos. Posidonius wrote that the nature of the whole ought to be apprehended by the *logos* that is akin to it.[19] Unfortunately, we do not have a similar statement in Chrysippus. In the area of 'sympathy' the writings of Chrysippus were overshadowed by those of Posidonius, and at the present time it is impossible to reconstruct the details of his doctrine.[20]

[18] For this sentence see Ps.-Plutarch, *De Fato*, ed. E. Valgiglio (Rome, 1964) 574 F, and notes on pp. 65-6. For the Stoic theory of cosmic sympathy see particularly Cicero, *De Natura Deorum*, ed. A.S. Pease (Harvard, 1958, repr. 1968) note on 2.19; and Cicero, *De Divinatione*, ed. A.S. Please, *University of Illinois Studies in Language and Literature* 6 (1920), 8 (1923, repr. 1963), note on 2.34, pp. 411-12.

[19] Theiler (1982) I F 461, II, pp. 402-4.

[20] For man's relation to the cosmos see particularly L. Edelstein, *The Meaning of Stoicism* (Harvard, 1966) 19-44. See also H. von Arnim, 'Die Stoische Lehre vom Fatum und Willensfreiheit', *Wissenschaftliche Beilage* 18, *Jahresbericht der Philosophischen Gesellschaft Universität Wien* (1905).

Appendix I

The Antecedents of the Stoic *Pragma*

The Stoic interpretation of speaking, namely that speaking is speaking a predicate which is a state of affairs, expressible and intelligible, may have been suggested by the arguments of the sophists. The first and most obvious place to look for the use of *pragma* with this meaning is a papyrus discovered in Egypt in 1941 attributed to the sophist Prodicus:

> Paradoxical is a certain judgment of Prodicus ... He states dogmatically 'It is not possible to contradict'. For, if they contradict, both are speaking. But it is impossible for both to speak with regard to the same *pragma*. For he says that only the man who speaks the truth and reports how the *pragmata* are is speaking. *But the man who opposes him is not speaking the pragma* ... His judgment is said to be paradoxical since it is contrary to the opinion of all.[1]

Commenting on the italicized sentence, Binder and Liesenborghs wrote: 'Beziehung auf unsicher.' They translated the sentence as: 'Dessen Widerpart aber spricht nicht ...'

[1] For the text see G. Binder and L. Liesenborghs, 'Eine Zuweisung der Sentenz *ouk estin antilegein* an Prodikos von Keos', *Mus. Helv.* 23 (1966) 37-43, repr. *Sophistik*, ed. C.J. Classen, *Wege der Forschung* 187 (Darmstadt, 1976) 452-62.

We can distinguish three ways in which the term *pragma* is used in this passage:

(a) Speaking a *pragma*.
(b) Speaking with regard to a *pragma*.
(c) Reporting how the *pragmata* are.

But only the last two can safely be attributed to Prodicus, and in both the term *pragma* may not denote anything more than an external object.

In this passage it is argued that it is impossible to contradict, because, if one of two men is reporting how the *pragmata* are, the other who is contradicting him is not reporting how the *pragmata* are. A passage in Plato's *Euthydemus* uses the term *pragma* in a manner similar to its use in the fragment of Prodicus. It is argued that contradiction is impossible (1) if two speakers speak a *logos* of the same *pragma*, (2) if neither speaks the *logos* of the *pragma*, (3) if one speaker speaks the *logos* of a *pragma*, but the other speaks a different *logos* of a different *pragma*, (4) if one speaks the *logos* of the *pragma* but the other speaks the *logos* of nothing at all (286a-b). At the end of the passage Socrates says:

> Although I have often heard this *logos* (i.e. that one cannot speak falsely) from many people on many occasions, I am always surprised at it ... Protagoras and his school used it a great deal and others of a still earlier period (286c).

It is doubtful whether the reference to Protagoras should be taken seriously. This interpretation of the *pragma* seems more in accord with the teachings of Prodicus, than with those of Protagoras. Socrates goes on to ask whether false opinion is possible even if speaking falsely is not, and the answer is in the negative (286d). Here it is argued that to speak means to speak a *logos*. The word *logos* appears to mean that account which expresses the nature of the *pragma*. The term *pragma* may refer to the external entity in this context. Since Antisthenes was influenced by Prodicus (Xen. *Symp.* 4.62), we would expect him to use the word *pragma* to denote a 'state of affairs', if, in fact, Prodicus had done so. The word *pragma* in Antisthenes, however, was used to denote an external entity, or thing.[2]

We shall have more success in finding a *pragma* which unmistakenly had the meaning 'state of affairs', if we turn to Gorgias' *Concerning Non-being*. We have two accounts of this. One is a summary by Sextus Empiricus in his *Adversus Mathematicos*,[3] and the other appears in the third part of a treatise erroneously attributed to Aristotle entitled *De Melisso, Xenophane, Gorgia*.[4] Using Newiger's text,[5] I shall provide a translation of a passage in the treatise:

> For it is necessary for all that is thought[6] to be, <if that-which-is is thought>[7] and for that-which-is-not, if it

[2] *Antisthenis Fragmenta*, collegit F.D. Caizzi (Milan, 1966) F 47A and 47B.

[3] S.E. *Math.* 7.65-87. Diels-Kranz 82 B 3.

[4] For a discussion of the text of this passage see H.J. Newiger, *Untersuchungen zu Gorgias' Schrift Über das Nichtseiende* (Berlin, 1973); J. Wiesner, *Ps.-Aristoteles MXG: Der Historische Wert des Xenophanesreferats. Beiträge zur Geschichte des Eleatismus* (Amsterdam, 1974); B. Cassin, *Si Parmenide. Cahiers de philologie* 4 (Lille, 1979). For a general discussion see G. Calogero, *Studi sull'Eleatismo* (Rome, 1932) 174-242; G.B. Kerferd, 'Gorgias on nature and that which is not', *Phronesis* 1 (1955) 3-25; W. Bröcker, 'Gorgias contra Parmenides', *Hermes* 86 (1958) 425-40; W. Luther, 'Wahrheit, Licht und Erkenntnis in der griechischen Philosophie bis Demokrit', *Arch. f. Begriffsgeschichte* 10 (1966) 223-7.

[5] Newiger (1973) 141.

[6] *ta phronoumena*. Regarding the verb *phroneô*, Newiger writes: 'Das verbum *phronein* muss bei Gorgias also ein geistiges Vermögen bezeichnen, das sowohl die sinnliche Wahrnehmung (*horan, akouein*) als auch das blosse Denken oder Imaginieren (*dianoeisthai*) umfasst. Wir geben es daher von nun an mit "vorstellen", *dianoeisthai* mit "bloss vorstellen" oder "bloss denken" wieder' (130).

[7] Newiger follows J. Cook Wilson, 'Apelt's Pseudo-Aristotelian treatises', *CR* 6 (1892) 17, in restoring *ei to on phroneitai*. The phrase is omitted in Cassin's text. See Newiger (1973) 141, n. 48a.

is not, not to be thought. But, if this is the case, no one can speak anything false, he says, not even if he should say[8] that chariots are engaging in a contest on the sea. For everything can be in this way. For whatever is seen and heard are for this reason: because each of them is thought. But if not for this reason but <because many people see the same things, those things which are seen are>; accordingly, what we see is, but it does not have a better claim to this term (sc. is) than what we conjecture.[9] For just as in that case many can see the same things, so in this case many can conjecture the same things <...> Whatever is true is not clear.[10] So that, even if they are, the *pragmata* cannot be recognized by us (980a9-18).[11]

Gorgias is stating two possible interpretations of 'that which is seen' and 'that which is heard': (1) They are because each of them is thought. 'That which is seen' and 'that which is heard' are 'that which is thought', and 'that which is thought' is that-which-is. Therefore, 'that which is seen', and 'that which is heard' are. (2) They are because many people see the same things. That which is seen, however, has no more claim to the predicate 'is' than that which is conjectured, since many people conjecture the same things. Since what is conjectured

[8] *Aristotelis quae feruntur ... De Melisso, Xenophane, Gorgia libellus*, ed. O. Apelt (Leipzig, 1888); *Aristotelis qui fertur de Melisso, Zenophane, Gorgia libellus*, ed. H. Diels, *Abh. der Kgl. Akad. Wiss. Berlin, Phil.-hist. Kl.* (Berlin, 1900); and Newiger (1973) 127, 141, all read *phaiê*. Cook Wilson (1892) 17, however, suggested *phronoiê* or *phaneiê*. Newiger (1973) 127, argued that *pseudes* before Aristotle could not be used to describe an act of thinking but was always connected with speaking.

[9] For 980a14-16 Cassin (1979) 515, read: *ei de mê dia touto, all' hôsper ouden mallon ha horômen estin, houtô mallon ha horômen ê dianooumetha.*

[10] For a discussion of *alêthes* (true) see A.P.D. Mourelatos, *The Route of Parmenides* (Yale, 1970) 63-7. The word may be best translated as 'that which is not hidden or concealed'.

[11] *agnôsta.* Snell argued that the verb *gignôskô* denoted the act of recognizing an object, as, for example, the recognition of a particular shape as a tree. The verb seems to have been associated with the act of seeing. See B. Snell, 'Die Ausdrücke für den Begriff des Wissens in der vorplatonischen Philosophie', *Ph. Unters.* 29 (1924) 21, cf. 48.

belongs to the class 'that which is thought', and 'that which is thought' is that-which-is, 'that which is seen' is also that-which-is. Gorgias is saying that either 'that which is seen' is identical with 'that which is thought' and with that-which-is, or it has the same claim to the predicate 'is' as 'that which is conjectured', which, in turn, is 'that which is thought'. On either interpretation 'that which is seen' is that-which-is.

What is the meaning of the term *pragmata* in the last sentence of this passage? It was, I believe, a state of affairs, such as 'that which is thought', 'that which is seen', 'that which is heard', and 'that which is conjectured'.

Evidence to support this interpretation of the term *pragmata* in Gorgias' *Concerning Non-being* is to be found elsewhere in the *De Melisso, Xenophane, Gorgia*:

> So that even if they are, *pragmata* cannot be known by us. If they can be known, he says, how can anyone reveal them to another person? For, he says, how can anyone express what he saw by means of the *logos*? How can this be clear to the man who hears it, if he has not seen it? For just as sight does not recognize sounds, so hearing does not recognize colours, but only sounds; and the man who speaks speaks, but he does not speak colour or the *pragma*. How can a man acquire an understanding of something of which he has no understanding from another man by a *logos* or some sign different from the *pragma* itself, unless in the case of a colour he can see it, or in the case of a sound he can hear it? No one expresses a sound or a colour at all, but *logos*; so that it is not possible to discern a colour but to see it, nor a sound but to hear it (980a19-b5) ... So that, if anything is, it cannot be known, and if it can be known, no one can reveal it to anyone else because *pragmata* are not *logoi*, and because no one acquires the same understanding as anyone else (980b15-8).

In this passage, the specifications for the *pragmata* are sounds and colours.

Sextus Empiricus has rewritten this section of Gorgias' *Concerning Non-being* so completely that very little of the original work is left. By eliminating words and concepts from later philosophy I can summarize the passage from Sextus Empiricus as follows:

> If it can be comprehended, it cannot be expressed to another person ... Those things that can be seen must be grasped by sight, and those things that can be heard by hearing, but not vice versa; how can these things be communicated to another person? (84). For that by which we communicate is *logos* ... Therefore, we do not communicate (sc. these) to our neighbour but *logos* ... (85) ... For from the flavour there arises the *logos* that is expressed about flavour and from the colour the *logos* about the colour (*Math.* 7.83-5).[12]

It is clear from the accounts in Sextus Empiricus and the *De Melisso, Xenophane, Gorgia* that what cannot be communicated is the object of sense perception. Sextus Empiricus calls these *ta onta* (those things-that-are); the passage in *De Melisso, Xenophane, Gorgia* refers to them as *pragmata*.

A passage in Plato's *Euthydemus* uses the term *pragma* to denote the subject of discussion. This seems to be a state of affairs, rather than an external entity:

> 'Well, Ctesippus,' said Euthydemus, 'do you think that it is possible to speak falsely?' 'Yes,' he said, 'if I have any sense at all.' 'And does one speak falsely when speaking the *pragma* (state of affairs?) which is the subject of discussion, or when not speaking it?' 'When speaking it.' 'Then, if he is speaking it itself, he is not speaking anything else that is than that which he is speaking, is he?' 'How is that?' said Ctesippus. 'What he is speaking is one part of that-which-is different from the rest.' 'Certainly.' 'Then, the man who speaks that speaks

---

[12] S.E. *Math.* 7.83-6 = Diels-Kranz 82 B 3 (83-6).

that-which-is,' he said. 'Yes.' 'But surely, that man who speaks that-which-is and those-things-which-are speaks the truth' (283e7 – 284a6).[13]

Euthydemus' position is this: If one spoke falsely, one would still speak and to speak is to speak that-which-is, but to speak that-which-is is to speak the truth; therefore, one cannot speak falsely.

Although the evidence is by no means conclusive, it seems to support the conclusion that the meaning which the Stoics attached to the term *pragma*, 'state of affairs', had already been given to it by Gorgias in his *Concerning Non-being*.

---

[13] For this passage see R.S.W. Hawtrey, *Commentary on Plato's Euthydemus* (American Philosophical Society, 1981) 98.

Appendix II

The Stoic Theory of Meaning

The Stoic theory of meaning belongs to a discussion of the Greek word *lexis*. This word is particularly difficult to translate because it denotes 'a group of letters which do not signify a predicate or a quality, and which may or may not indicate one or more meanings'. As a specification for a group of letters which do not signify a meaning we have *blituri* (3.20, p. 213). A *lexis* which indicates may be spoken or written.[1] The Stoic *lexis* formed the basis for their discussion of anomaly and amphiboly.

Varro's *De Lingua Latina* has a sentence which reads:

> For Chrysippus, when he writes about the anomaly of words, intends to demonstrate that similar things are denoted by dissimilar words and that dissimilar things are denoted by similar words (2.151).

Dahlmann based his interpretations of these lines on the Stoic view that the form of a word was often inconsistent with that which is indicated by it. He wrote: 'Die Anomalie ist für ihn (sc. Chrysippus) die Feststellung einer Unstimmigkeit zwischen der lautlichen Form

---

[1] For the *lexis* see R. Haller, 'Untersuchungen zum Bedeutungsproblem in der antiken und mittelalterlichen Philosophie', *Arch. f. Begriffsgeschichte* 7 (1962) 81-5.

und dem Sinne des bennanten Objektes.'[2] His interpretation was adopted by Barwick in his *Probleme der Stoischen Sprachlehre und Rhetorik*,[3] although earlier in his *Remmius Palaemon und die Römische Ars Grammatica*[4] he had argued that the sentence in Varro should be interpreted in the light of the Stoic premise that an anomaly arose when the same idea was expressed through different words or when the same word expressed different ideas. Dahlmann's interpretation was accepted by Frede.[5]

A passage in Simplicius illustrates the inconsistency between the form of a word and its meaning:

> And furthermore, we should realize that sometimes words which do not express privation indicate privation, as, for example, 'poverty' (*penia*) indicates the privation of property and 'blind man' (*tuphlos*) indicates the privation of sight. But sometimes words which express privation do not indicate privation. For 'immortal' (*athanatos*), although it has the form of the *lexis* which expresses privation, does not signify privation ... Since the anomaly is great, Chrysippus in his book *Concerning those things which express privation* investigated it thoroughly (2.177, p. 52).

The problem was probably discussed by Chrysippus also in his *Concerning the Anomaly in the lexeis* (*SVF* 2, p. 6, 111).

---

[2] H. Dahlmann, *Varro und die Hellenistische Sprachtheorie* (Berlin, 1932, repr. 1964) 53.

[3] K. Barwick, 'Probleme der Stoischen Sprachtheorie und Rhetorik', *Abh. Sächs. Akad. Wiss. Leipzig, Phil.-hist. Kl.* 49,3 (Berlin, 1957) 54.

[4] K. Barwick, *Remmius Palaemon und die Römische Ars Grammatica* (Leipzig, 1922) 179.

[5] M. Frede, 'Principles of Stoic grammar', in *The Stoics*, ed. J.M. Rist (California, 1978) 72-3.

A passage in Apollonius Dyscolus' *Concerning Conjunctions*, which, as Dahlmann argued,[6] shows Stoic influence, is similar:

> We say that *machomai* (I fight) is passive, and it is clear that it is in the form of the articulate sound. Yet if it is considered in the light of what is indicated (*to dêloumenon*), it is clear that it is active. Furthermore, *paidion* (child) is neuter because of its form, although it is both (sc. masculine and feminine) because of what is indicated ... And *Thêbai* (Thebes) is plural, but the city is one.

Diogenes Laertius' definition of amphiboly suggests a very different topic for discussion:

> Amphiboly is a *lexis* which signifies two or more *pragmata* verbally and properly and according to the same custom so that it is possible to accept several at the same time in conformity with the same *lexis*, as, for example, *aulêtrispeptôke*. For one thing is indicated by it, as, for example, *oikia tris peptôke* (a house has fallen three times), and another, as, for example, *autêtris peptôke* (a flute-girl has fallen, 3.23, p.214).

The same specification is used in the first Stoic amphiboly in Galen's *On Fallacies due to Language*.[7]

> The first (sc. amphiboly) is that which they call common to what is strung along and what is divided, as, for example, *AULÊTRISPESOUSA*. For it is common to *aulêtris* as a word and as divided.

[6] Dahlmann (1932, 1964) 52. Apollonius Dyscolus, *Concerning Conjunctions*, 215, 18-216, 1.

[7] R.B. Edlow, *Galen on Language and Ambiguity* (Leiden, 1977) 106.

In this specification, *AULÊTRISPESOUSA* is a common *lexis* for the *lexeis, aulêtris pesousa* and *aulê tris pesousa*. The former may be translated as 'a flute-girl having fallen', and the latter as 'a house having fallen three times'.

When Diogenes Laertius wrote that 'amphiboly is a *lexis* which signifies two or more *pragmata*', he was using the word *pragmata* to denote one or more meanings indicated by the *lexis*. A definition of anomaly in Gellius is similar to Diogenes Laertius' definition of amphiboly: *Chrysippus ait omne verbum ambiguum natura esse, quoniam ex eodem duo vel plura accipi possunt* (2.152). This may be translated as: 'Chrysippus says that every word is anomalous by nature, because from the same word two or more (?) can be understood.' Since the words *duo vel plura* (two or more) are neuter, they may represent either *pragmata* or *ta dêloumena* (those things which are indicated).

The evidence for the Stoic synonym is much more difficult to interpret. A passage in Simplicius reads:

> Aristotle called those things which have the same definition along with the name synonyms, more appropriately than the Stoics who called those things that have many names at the same time (*ta polla hama echonta onomata*) synonyms, as, for example, Paris and Alexander are the same, and simply the so-called polyonems (*In Cat.* p. 36,8-12 = 2.150).[8]

The Stoics did not accept Aristotle's definition of a synonym, because they did not accept his definition of a definition. Aristotle held that an entity should be defined in terms of the genus and the differentia (*Top.* 141b28-9).

---

[8] The Stoic definition of a synonym may be preserved in a quotation from Stephanus by the Scholiast on the *Grammar of Dionysius Thrax*: 'A synonym is the substratum for one substance in several names, as, for example, *merops* (articulate), *brotos* (mortal), *anthrôpos* (man) which the Peripatetics call homonyms' (Bekker (1816, 1965) 868,14-16).

Chrysippus defined a definition as 'the assigning of the essential characteristic' (*idion*, 2.226); Antipater of Tarsus as 'a *logos* expressed adequately by resolution' (ibid.). Alexander tells us, however, that there was no difference between the two definitions (3.24, p. 247).

The individual quality was indicated by the proper name (3.22, p. 213). It is clear, therefore, that the proper names 'Paris' and 'Alexander' in the passage from Simplicius quoted above signified individual qualities in a common substratum. Simplicius writes: 'The Stoics who called those things that have many names at the same time synonyms.' The words 'those things that have many names at the same time' must refer to the qualifications (*poia*) or to the individually qualified entities in which the qualifications reside. Since the definition was 'the assigning of the essential characteristic' to the qualification, and since each individual quality was formed from one essential characteristic, the qualities denoted by the names 'Paris' and 'Alexander' could not have the same essential characteristic or the same definition.[9]

Tarán, however, found the passage in Simplicius absurd. Commenting on Simplicius, *In Cat.* p. 36,9-12 (2.150), Tarán wrote:

That the Stoics defined *synonyma* as a property of *onomata*, not of things, as Simplicius wrongly thinks, is clear not only because of the absurdity Simplicius assigns to them, but also because of Boethus' comments on the moderns' use of *synonyma* (*In Cat.* p. 36, 28-30) and on the ancients' use of it (*In Cat.* p. 38,22-3); the Stoics must have said that *synonyma* are words which have the same meaning.[10]

[9] M.E. Reesor, 'The Stoic *idion* and Prodicus' near-synonyms', *AJP* 104 (1983) 124-9.

[10] L. Tarán, 'Speusippus and Aristotle on homonymy and synonymy', *Hermes* 106 (1978) 86, n. 39.

The first passage to which Tarán refers (p. 36,25-31) may be translated as follows:

> Where, then, our investigation is concerned with several articulate sounds and many kinds of naming for each thing, just as in the *Poetics* and the third book of the *Rhetoric*, we need the other kind of synonym which Speusippus called a polyonem, and *Boethus was incorrect when he said that what are called synonyms by the moderns were omitted by Aristotle, I mean, what Speusippus called polyonems, for they were not omitted, but they were taken up in other studies in which the discussion was appropriate.*

Boethus of Sidon was a Peripatetic philosopher who lived in the second part of the first century BC and wrote a commentary on Aristotle's *Categories*. Tarán has argued convincingly that Simplicius knew Boethus only through Porphyry.[11] On p. 36,25-31, Simplicius quotes a passage from Porphyry's *To Gedaleias* in which Porphyry refers to Boethus and Speusippus. Porphyry was born in Tyre about AD 232 and died early in the fourth century. There is little doubt that the moderns to whom Porphyry refers are Stoics. As Barnes pointed out, Alexander of Aphrodisias used the term 'moderns' to refer to the Stoics.[12]

Tarán argued that Porphyry had in mind Aristotle's remarks concerning a synonym in the *Rhetoric*:

> Of words homonyms are useful to the sophist (for he misleads people with these) and synonyms to the poet, I mean ordinary words with the same meaning, as, for example, *to poreuesthai* (to proceed) and *to badizein* (to go). For these two are ordinary words and have the same meaning (*Rhet.* 1404b37-1450a2).

[11] ibid. 78-9. See also L. Tarán, *Speusippus of Athens* (Leiden, 1981) 407.
[12] J. Barnes, 'Homonymy in Aristotle and Speusippus', *CQ* n.s. 21 (1971) 70, n. 4.

It is perfectly possible, however, that Boethus was correct in saying that 'what are called synonyms by the moderns were omitted by Aristotle'.
How did Speusippus define the term polyonem? Here, we have to turn to the second passage to which Tarán refers, a passage in Simplicius' *Commentary on Aristotle's Categories* which reads:

> *Boethus tells us, then, that Speusippus adopted such a diaeresis since it included all words (onomata). Of words, he says, some are tautonyms, others heteronyms (we understand the synonyms according to the custom of the ancients); of the heteronyms some are peculiarly heteronyms, others are polyonems, and others are paronyms.* An account of the others has been given (p. 38,19-24).

It is clear, as Barnes and Tarán have argued, that the source of the passage which begins: 'An account of the others has been given' is not Speusippus. Barnes said that it was Boethus;[13] Tarán that it was Simplicius.[14] The references to heteronyms and polyonems in the passage cannot be attributed to Speusippus. I believe that Tarán is right in believing that *phêsi* (he says) refers to Speusippus.[15] The word *hêmôn* (we) in the parenthesis may be 'Boethus and his contemporaries', as Barnes stated,[16] or 'Boethus', as Tarán held.[17] The parenthesis may appear to indicate that Speusippus' synonyms were identical with Aristotle's synonyms.

The nature of Speusippus' linguistic terms has recently been the subject of a very lively debate between Barnes and Tarán. Barnes argued that Speusippus followed

---

[13] ibid. 69.
[14] Tarán (1978) 82; Tarán (1981) 410-1.
[15] Tarán (1978) 80; Tarán (1981) 409-10. Barnes (1971) 69 argued that it was Boethus.
[16] Barnes (1971) 69.
[17] Tarán (1978) 80; Tarán (1981) 409. See also E. Heitsch, 'Die Entdeckung der Homonymie', *Akad. Wiss. und Literatur, Mainz. Abh. der Geistes— und Sozialwissenschaften Klasse*, nr. 11 (1972) 49.

Aristotle in regarding synonyms as 'things'; Tarán that he classified names. The question is relevant to this chapter only if we accept Porphyry's statement that what the Stoics called synonyms were called polyonems by Speusippus (*In Cat.* p. 36,29-31). Since I am inclined to agree with Boethus' assertion that 'what are called synonyms by the moderns (i.e. the Stoics) were omitted by Aristotle' (ibid.), I am convinced that it is pointless to try to decide how the Stoics regarded synonyms on the basis of the evidence for Speusippus' polyonemy, tenuous as it is.

Bibliography

Editions of ancient works cited

Diogenis Laertii, *Vitae Philosophorum*, 2 vols, ed. H.S. Long (Oxford, 1964).

Doxographi Graeci, ed. H. Diels (Berlin, 1879, repr. De Gruyter, 1976).

Galen, *On the Doctrines of Hippocrates and Plato*, ed. with translation, and commentary by P. De Lacy, 3 vols (*Corpus Medicorum Graecorum* V 4,1,2, Berlin, 1980-4).

Plutarch, *Moralia*, XIII, part II, ed. H. Cherniss (Loeb, Harvard, 1976).

Posidonius, vol. 1. *The Fragments*, ed. L. Edelstein and I.G. Kidd (Cambridge, 1972).

Poseidonios, *Die Fragmente* I und II, ed. W. Theiler (Berlin, 1982).

Pseudo-Andronicus de Rhodes, *Peri Pathôn*, ed. A. Glibert-Thirry (Leiden, 1977).

Simplicius, *In Aristotelis Categorias Commentarium*, ed. C. Kalbfleisch *CAG* VIII (Berlin, 1907).

Stobaeus, *Eclogae Physicae et Ethicae*, ed. C. Wachsmuth, 4 vols (Berlin, 1908, repr. 1974).

Stoicorum Veterum Fragmenta, ed. H. von Arnim, 3 vols (Stuttgart, 1903, repr. 1964), vol. 4, Indices, ed. M. Adler (Stuttgart, 1924, repr. 1964).

Collected essays

Doubt and Dogmatism. Studies in Hellenistic Epistemology, ed. M. Schofield, M. Burnyeat, J. Barnes (Oxford, 1980).

Language and Logos. Studies in Ancient Greek Philosophy, ed. M. Schofield, M. Nussbaum (Cambridge, 1982).

The Norms of Nature. Studies in Hellenstic Ethics, ed. M. Schofield, G. Striker (Cambridge, 1986).

On Stoic and Peripatetic Ethics. The Work of Arius Didymus, ed. W.W. Fortenbaugh. *Rutgers University Studies in Classical Humanities* 1 (New Brunswick, N.J., 1983).

Problems in Stoicism, ed. A.A. Long (London, 1971).
Science and Speculation. Studies in Hellenistic Theory and Practice,
    ed. J. Barnes, J. Brunschwig, M. Burnyeat, M. Schofield (Cambridge, 1982).
The Skeptical Tradition, ed. M. Burnyeat (California, 1983).
Les stoïciens et leur logique, ed. J. Brunschwig (Paris, 1978).
The Stoics, ed. J.M. Rist (California, 1978).

Select bibliography

Adorno, F. (1959) 'Sul significato del termine *hêgemonikon* in Zenone Stoico', *La Parola del Passato. Rivista di Studi Classici* 14, 26-41.

Alpers-Gölz, R. (1976) *Der Begriff Skopos in der Stoa und seine Vorgeschichte*, Hildesheim.

Annas, J. (1980) 'Truth and knowledge', in *Doubt and Dogmatism*, Oxford, 84-104.

Arthur, E.P. (1983) 'The Stoic analysis of the mind's reactions to presentations', *Hermes* III, 69-78.

Barnes, J. (1971) 'Homonymy in Aristotle and Speusippus' *CQ* n.s. 21, 65-80.

Barnes, J. (1978) 'La doctrine du retour éternel', in *Les stoïciens et leur logique*, 3-20.

Blank, D.L. (1981) *Ancient Philosophy and Grammar. American Classical Studies* 10, Scholar's Press, California.

Bloos, L. (1973) *Probleme der Stoischen Physik*, Hamburg.

Bonhöffer, A. (1894, repr. 1968), *Epictet und die Stoa*, Stuttgart.

Bréhier, E. (1951) *Chrysippe et l'ancien stoïcisme*², Paris.

Brink, C.O. (1956) '*Oikeiôsis* and *oikeiôtês*. Theophrastus and Zeno on Nature in moral theory', *Phronesis* 1, 123-45.

Brunschwig, J. (1986) 'The cradle argument', in *The Norms of Nature*, Cambridge, 128-44.

Burnyeat, M.F. (1982) 'The origins of non-deductive inference', in *Science and Speculation*, Cambridge, 193-238.

Cassin, B. (1979) *Si Parmenide*, Lille.

Charles, D. (1984) *Aristotle's Philosophy of Action*, Ithaca, N.Y.

Couissin, P. (1929) 'Le stoïcisme de la nouvelle académie', *Rev. d'Histoire de la Philosophie* 3, 241-76, repr. (1983) 'The Stoicism of the New Academy', in *The Skeptical Tradition*, California, 31-51.

De Lacy, P. (1945) 'The Stoic categories as methodological principles', *TAPA* 76, 246-63.

De Lacy, P.H. (1983) 'Comments on Professor Kidd's paper', in *On Stoic and Peripatetic Ethics*, 114-17.

Delamarre, Alexandre J.-L. (1980) 'La notion de *ptôsis* chez Aristote et les stoïciens', in *Concepts et catégories dans la pensée antique*, ed. P. Aubenque, Paris, 321-45.

Detel, W. *et al.* (1980) *'Lekta ellipê* in der Stoischen Sprachphilosophie', *Arch. Gesch. Phil.* 62, 276-88.

Dörrie, H. (1955) 'Hypostasis Wort- und Bedeutungsgeschichte', *Nach. Akad. Wiss. Göttingen Phil.-hist. Kl.* 1, 3, 35-92.

Dragona-Monachou, M. (1976) *The Stoic Arguments for the Existence and Providence of the Gods*, Athens.

Edelstein, L. (1966) *The Meaning of Stoicism*, Harvard.

Edlow, R.B. (1977) *Galen on Language and Ambiguity*, Leiden.

Edwards, M.W. (1960) 'The expression of Stoic ideas in the *Aeneid'*, *Phoenix* 14, 151-65.

Elorduy, E. (1972) *El Estoicismo* I and II, Madrid.

Engberg-Pedersen, T. (1986) 'Discovering the good; *oikeiôsis* and *kathêkonta* in Stoic ethics', in *The Norms of Nature*, Cambridge, 145-83.

Forschner, M. (1980) 'Die pervierte Vernunft. Zur Stoischen Theorie der Affekte', *Philosophisches Jahrbuch*, 87, 258-80.

Forschner, M. (1981) *Die Stoische Ethik: über den Zusammenhang von Natur-Sprach- und Moralphilosophie im altstoischen System*, Stuttgart.

Frede, M. (1974) *Die Stoische Logik*, Göttingen.

Frede, M. (1978) 'Principles of Stoic grammar', in *The Stoics*, California, 27-75.

Frede, M. (1980) 'The original notion of cause', in *Doubt and Dogmatism*, Oxford, 217-49.

Frede, M. (1986) 'The Stoic doctrine of the affections of the soul', in *The Norms of Nature*, Cambridge, 93-110.

Furley, D.J. (1966) 'Lucretius and the Stoics', *Bulletin of the Institute of Classical Studies. London University* 13, 13-33.

Gill, C. (1983) 'Did Chrysippus understand Medea?' *Phronesis* 28, 136-49.

Glibert-Thirry, A. (1977) 'La théorie stoïcienne de la passion chez Chrysippe et son évolution chez Posidonius', *Revue Philosophique de Louvain* 75, 393-435

Görler, W. (1977) *'Asthenês Sunkatathesis.* Zur Stoischen Erkenntnistheorie', *Würzburger Jahrbücher für die Altertumswissenschaft* N.F. III, 83-92.

Görler, W. (1984) 'Zum virtus-fragment des Lucilius (1326-1338 Marx) und zur Geschichte der Stoischen Güterlehre', *Hermes* 112, 445-68.

Goldschmidt, V. (1972) *'Huparchein* et *huphistanai* dans la philosophie stoicienne', *REG* 85, 331-44.

Gosling, J.C.B. and Taylor, C.C.W. (1982) 'The stoics', in *The Greeks on*

Pleasure, Oxford, 415-27.

Gould, J.B. (1970) *The Philosophy of Chrysippus*, Leiden.

Graeser, A. (1971) 'A propos *huparchein* bei den Stoikern', *Arch. f. Begriffsgeschichte* 15, 299-305.

Graeser, A. (1972) *Plotinus and the Stoics. A Preliminary Study*, Leiden.

Graeser, A. (1975) *Zenon von Kition. Positionen und Probleme*, Berlin.

Graeser, A. (1977) 'On language, thought and reality in ancient Greek philosophy', *Dialectica* 31, 359-88.

Graeser, A. (1978a) 'The Stoic theory of meaning', in *The Stoics*, California, 77-100.

Graeser, A. (1978b) 'The Stoic categories', in *Les stoiciens et leur logique*, Paris, 199-221.

Hadot, P. (1966) 'La notion de "cas" dans la logique stoïcienne', *Le Langage. Actes du XIIIᵉ congrès des sociétés de philosophie de langue française*, Neuchâtel, 109-12.

Hadot, P. (1969) 'Zur Vorgeschichte des Briffs "Existenz" *huparchein* bei den Stoikern', *Arch. f. Begriffsgeschichte* 13, 115-27.

Hadot, P. (1980) 'Sur divers sens du mot *pragma* dans la tradition philosophique grecque', in *Concepts et catégories dans la pensée antique*, ed. P. Aubenque, Paris, 309-19.

Hahm, D.E. (1977) *The Origins of Stoic Cosmology*, Ohio.

Heinrichs, A. (1974) 'Die Kritik der Stoischen Theologie im PHerc. 1428', *Cronache Ercolanesi* 4, 5-32.

Heinze, R. (1872, repr. 1961) *Die Lehre vom Logos in der Griechischen Philosophie*, Berlin.

Heitsch, E. (1972) 'Die Entdeckung der Homonymie', *Akad. Wiss. und Lit. Mainz. Abh. der Geistes- und Sozialwissenschaftlichen Klasse*, nr. 11, 22-88.

Hossenfelder, M. (1967) 'Zur Stoischen Definition von Axioma', *Arch. f. Begriffsgeschichte* 11, 238-41.

Imbert, C. (1978) 'Théorie de la représentation et doctrine logique dans le stoïcisme ancien', in *Les stoïciens et leur logique*, Paris, 223-49.

Imbert, C. (1980) 'Stoic logic and Alexandrian poetics', in *Doubt and Dogmatism*, Oxford, 182-216.

Inwood, B. (1984) 'Hierocles: theory and argument in the second century A.D.', *Oxford Studies in Ancient Philosophy* 2, 151-83.

Inwood, B. (1985) *Ethics and Human Action in Early Stoicism*, Oxford.

Irwin, T.H. (1986) 'Stoic and Aristotelian conceptions of happiness', in *The Norms of Nature*, Cambridge, 205-44.

Kerferd, G.B. (1972a) 'The search for personal identity in Stoic thought', *Bulletin of the John Rylands University Library of Manchester* 55, 177-96.

Kerferd, G.B. (1972b) 'Cicero and Stoic ethics', in *Cicero and Virgil. Studies in Honour of Harold Hunt*, ed. J.R.C. Martyn, Amsterdam, 60-74.

Kerferd, G.B. (1978a) 'What does the Wise Man know?', in *The Stoics*, California, 125-36.

Kerferd, G.B. (1978b) 'The problem of *synkatathesis* and *katalepsis* in Stoic doctrine', in *Les stoïciens et leur logique*, Paris, 250-72.

Kerferd, G.B. (1978c) 'The origin of evil in Stoic thought', *Bulletin of the John Rylands University Library of Manchester* 60, 482-94.

Kerferd, G.B. (1982) 'Two problems concerning impulses', in *On Stoic and Peripatetic Ethics*, New Brunswick, N.J., 87-98.

Kidd, I.G. (1971) 'The Stoic intermediates and the end for man', in *Problems in Stoicism*, London, 150-72.

Kidd, I.G. (1978) 'Moral actions and rules in Stoic ethics', in *The Stoics*, California, 247-58.

Kidd, I.G. (1983) '*Euemptôsia* – proneness to disease', in *On Stoic and Peripatetic Ethics*, New Brunswick, N.J., 107-13.

Lapidge, M. (1973) 'A problem in Stoic cosmology', *Phronesis* 18, 240-78.

Lapidge, M. (1978) 'Stoic cosmology', in *The Stoics*, California, 161-85.

Lloyd, A.C. (1970) 'Activity and description in Aristotle and the Stoa', *Dawes Hicks Lecture on Philosophy. Proceedings of the British Academy* 56 (1970) 3-16.

Lloyd, A.C. (1971) 'Grammar and metaphysics in the Stoa', in *Problems in Stoicism*, London, 58-74.

Lloyd, A.C. (1978a) 'Definite propositions and the concept of reference', in *Les stoïciens et leur logique*, Paris, 285-95.

Lloyd, A.C. (1978b) 'Emotion and decision in Stoic psychology', in *The Stoics*, California, 233-46.

Long, A.A. (1967) 'Carneades and the Stoic Telos', *Phronesis* 12, 59-90.

Long, A.A. (1968) 'The Stoic concept of evil', *Philosophical Quarterly* 18, 329-43.

Long, A.A. (1971a) 'Language and thought in Stoicism', in *Problems in Stoicism*, London, 75-113.

Long, A.A. (1971b) 'Freedom and determinism in the Stoic theory of human action', in *Problems in Stoicism*, London, 173-99.

Long, A.A. (1974) *Hellenistic Philosophy*, London.

Long, A.A. (1976) 'The early Stoic concept of moral choice', in *Images of Man in Ancient and Medieval Thought. Studia Gerardo Verbeke*, Leuven, 77-92.

Long, A.A. (1978) 'The Stoic distinction between truth (*hê alêtheia*) and the true (*to alêthes*)', in *Les stoïciens et leur logique*, Paris, 297-315.

Long, A.A. and Sedley, D.N. (1987) *The Hellenistic Philosophers* 1 and 2, Cambridge.

Longrigg, J. (1975) 'Elementary physics in the Lyceum and the Stoa', *Isis* 66, 211-29.

Mansfeld, J. (1979) 'Providence and the destruction of the universe in early Stoic thought', in *Studies in Hellenistic Religion*, ed. M.J. Vermaseren, Leiden 129-88.

Mates, B. (1953, 1961) *Stoic Logic*², California.

Mühl, M. (1962) 'Der *logos endiathetos* und *prophorikos* von der älteren Stoa bis zur Synode von Sirmium 351', *Arch. f. Begriffsgeschichte* 7, 7-56.

Newiger, H.J. (1973) *Untersuchungen zu Gorgias' Schrift über das Nichtseiende*, Berlin.

Pasquino, P. (1978) 'Le statut ontologique des incorporels dans l'ancien stoicisme', in *Les stoïciens et leur logique*, Paris, 375-86.

Pembroke, S.G. (1971) '*Oikeiôsis*', in *Problems in Stoicism*, London, 114-49.

Pohlenz, M. (1938) 'Zenon und Chrysipp', *Nach. Ges. Wiss. Göttingen, Phil.-hist. Kl.* NF 2, 9, 173-210.

Pohlenz, M. (1939) 'Die Begründung der abendländischen Sprachlehre durch die Stoa', *Nach. Ges. Wiss. Göttingen, Phil.-hist. Kl.* NF 3, 6, 151-98.

Pohlenz, M. (1940) 'Grundfragen der Stoischen Philosophie', *Abh. Ges. Wiss. Göttingen, Phil.-hist. Kl.* 3, 26, 1-81.

Pohlenz, M. (1970-2) *Die Stoa*,⁴ Göttingen

Reesor, M.E. (1951a) *The Political Theory of the Old and Middle Stoa*, New York.

Reesor, M.E. (1951b) 'The "indifferents" in the Old and Middle Stoa', *TAPA* 82, 102-10.

Reesor, M.E. (1954) 'The Stoic concept of quality', *AJP* 75, 40-58.

Reesor, M.E. (1957) 'The Stoic categories', *AJP* 78, 63-82.

Reesor, M.E. (1965) 'Fate and possibility in early Stoic philosophy', *Phoenix* 19, 285-97.

Reesor, M.E. (1970) 'The Stoics', in *Encyclopaedia Britannica*.

Reesor, M.E. (1972) '*Poion* and *poiotês* in Stoic philosophy', *Phronesis* 17, 279-85.

Reesor, M.E. (1978) 'Necessity and fate in Stoic philosophy', in *The Stoics*, California, 187-202.

Reesor, M.E. (1983a) 'On the Stoic Goods in Stobaeus, *Eclogae* 2', in *On Stoic and Peripatetic Ethics*, New Brunswick, N.J., 75-84.

Reesor, M.E. (1983b) 'The Stoic *idion* and Prodicus' near-synonyms', *AJP* 104, 124-33.

Rieth, O. (1933) *Grundbegriffe der Stoischen Ethik. Problemata* 9, Berlin.

Rist, J.M. (1969) *Stoic Philosophy*, Cambridge.

Rist, J.M. (1971) 'Categories and their uses', in *Problems in Stoicism*, London, 38-57.

Sambursky, S. (1959) *Physics of the Stoics*, London.

Sandbach, F.H. (1971a) '*Phantasia kataléptiké*', in *Problems in Stoicism*, London, 9-21.

Sandbach, F.H. (1971b) *'Ennoia* and *prolêpsis* in the Stoic theory of knowledge', in *Problems in Stoicism*, London, 22-37.

Sandbach, F.H. (1975) *The Stoics*, London.

Sandbach, F.H. (1985) *Aristotle and the Stoics. The Cambridge Philological Society* Suppl. vol. 10.

Sedley, D. (1982a) 'The Stoic criterion of identity', *Phronesis*, 27, 255-75.

Sedley, D. (1982b) 'Comments on Professor Reesor's paper', in *On Stoic and Peripatetic Ethics*, New Brunswick, N.J., 85-6.

Solmsen, F. (1968) 'Cleanthes or Posidonius? The basis of Stoic physics', in *Kleine Schriften* 1, Hildesheim, 436-60.

Stannard, J.W. (1958) *The Psychology of the Passions in the Old Stoa*. Ph.D. Dissertation, University of Illinois.

Striker, G. (1974) *'Kriterion tês alêtheias'*, *Nach. Akad. Wiss. Göttingen Phil.-hist. Kl.* 1,2.

Striker, G. (1983) 'The role of *oikeiôsis* in Stoic ethics', *Oxford Studies in Ancient Philosophy* 1, 145-67.

Striker, G. (1986) 'Antipater, or the art of living', in *The Norms of Nature*, Cambridge, 185-204.

Tarán, L. (1978) 'Speusippus and Aristotle on homonymy and synonymy', *Hermes* 106, 73-99.

Tarán, L. (1981) *Speusippus of Athens*, Leiden.

Todd, R.B. (1976) *Alexander of Aphrodisias on Stoic Physics*, Leiden.

Todd, R.B. (1978) 'Monism and immanence: the foundations of Stoic physics', in *The Stoics*, California, 137-60.

Tsekourakis, D. (1974) *Studies in the Terminology of Early Stoic Ethics. Hermes Einzelschriften* 32, Wiesbaden.

Verbeke, G. (1945) *L'évolution de la doctrine du pneuma du Stoïcisme à S. Augustin*, Louvain.

Verbeke, G. (1977) 'Der Nominalismus der Stoischen Logik', *Allgemeine Zeitschrift für Philosophie* 11, 36-55.

Voelke, A.-J. (1973) *L'idée de volonté dans le stoïcisme*, Paris.

Von Staden, H. (1978) 'The Stoic theory of perception and its "Platonic" critics', in *Studies in Perception*, ed. F.K. Machamer and R.G. Turnbull, Ohio, 96-136.

Watson, G. (1966) *The Stoic Theory of Knowledge*, Belfast.

White, M.J. (1980) 'Aristotle's temporal interpretation of necessary coming-to-be and Stoic determinism', *Phoenix* 34, 208-18.

White, N.P. (1978) 'Two notes on Stoic terminology' *AJP* 99, 111-19.

White, N.P. (1979) 'The basis of Stoic ethics', *HSCP* 83, 143-78.

Index of Modern Authors

171

Subject Index